WRITING IN AMERICA

ERSKINE CALDWELL

WRITING IN AMERICA

PHAEDRA PUBLISHERS, NEW YORK

808.02

CONTENTS:

INTRODUCTION

The marketplace for the exchange of reading and writing is a crowded bazaar of bargaining and barter. The bidding for reading matter is always brisk and an offering of some kind of written material is always available. Like any shrewd trader, the expert reader has a sure knowledge of the true values of literature and willingly pays a higher price for superior quality. The novice or inexperienced reader is always an easy mark for the beguiling pitchman and is likely to become the victim of his own ignorance and pay dearly for inferior quality. He is the buyer who should beware of deception.

An expert reader is a perceptive person who knows exactly what he wishes to read and he knows how to find his way to the books of his choice. Due to his training and discernment, his judgment is keen and objective, and he is not easily misled or flustered by fashions and fads and transitory popularity. He is the buyer who is aware of true values.

Such a reader knows that a person does not have the physical endurance to read everything that is written, and certainly not the desire to do so. Furthermore, he knows that by using judicious judgment he has the practical qualifications to make his own decisions and not be influenced by selections other readers might make.

In order to attain this eminence of being an expert reader, such a person will have acquired along the way a mastery of the art of reading to no less a degree than the author who has mastered the art of writing. Consequently, the expert reader will be able to appreciate and appraise literary values much better than a person who might read the same books merely because they are intellectually fashionable or socially popular. Speed reading or scanning a five-hundred-page novel in forty-five minutes might win a contest, but it would never contribute to anyone's enjoyment or education.

One of the prerequisite and most important steps to be taken by anyone who has the desire to become an expert reader is to acquire the knowledge and ability to question and evaluate the literary notions that constantly appear in the guise of intellectualism as well as those which suddenly become popular and widespread. Preciousness in reading can become as prosaic as over-simplification in writing.

In the world of reading and writing there are literary notions that might be defined as being atmospheric ideas or pervading influences that are generated and diffused by individual and collective thinking. The source of these notions is not always apparent; often they just suddenly appear out of the blue.

Such ideas or notions, regardless of whether they are considered to be good or bad in social, economic, political, or literary effect, do initiate and propagate the trend of the times, the fashions of an era, the mores of a generation, and the traditions of civilization. Some of these ideas and influences are quickly dissipated before they can appear in print, and the more appealing and effective ones that linger in the collective mind are always recorded in print. One and all, these literary fashions are as subject to whimsical mutation as the faddish tilt of a man's hat and the modish hemline of a woman's skirt.

The establishment of any idea or notion which induces the acceptance of dubious literary values by a majority of readers and writers always results in conformity of thought and a stubborn resistance to individual expression. Personal thoughts or individual ideas, as distinct from collective notions, are generally looked upon as being suspiciously radical, seditious, or anti-social.

Only the strong-willed and most dedicated writers and critics of writing have the courage and ability to reject the conservative and reactionary ideas of the past and to free themselves from conforming attitudes. Such writers and critics are easily identified. They are the ones who do not hesitate to make known their credos, past and present, and to propound their visions of the future.

The purpose of this volume of personal notions is to present some individualistic thoughts and ideas on the subject of reading and writing. As a result, it is hoped that it will reveal, to the best of my ability and to the extent of my experience, some of the prevailing ills and complaints of fiction, as well as to suggest its healthy potential.

Since there is no infallible guide to perfected writing and no guaranteed handbook of successful authorship—at least to my knowledge there is none—it would be an iniquitous act on my part to intimate that there might be such helpful aids in existence. And advice about how to write a short story or novel has become just about as impractable and frustrating as advocating the short word in preference to the long word regardless of the meaning to be defined. Only the writer himself knows the exact shading of meaning most suitable and expressive of what he is saying.

It is to be hoped, above all, that the daredevils of the typewriter—those perennially youthful pioneers who have no fear of exploring new frontiers—will find here the suggestion and urge to seek more distant boundaries of reading and writing. As to be expected, some of the workers of the printed page will make the choice of being content with my findings. Others will accept the challenge to disagree with my conclusions and set out to seek their own ideals.

If the literary notions of the times are to be revised, it will be the inquiring minds and daredevils of the typewriter who will do it. It is they who have the courage to display personal thoughts and new concepts of fiction, as well as having the ability to create their ideal of it.

The ideals of fiction and the philosophies of the novel do change year by year as surely as the calendar is to be turned day by day. Although masterpieces of literature remain as monuments to the past, and will continue to be respected as such, there exists, nevertheless, the artistic necessity for constant revisions of fashions in reading and styles of writing. The artistry of storytelling has always made its own rules and regulations, and reserved the right to make changes without notice.

Storytelling on the printed page will continue to be a lively art as long as the following sequence takes place:

First, a group of persons will conduct themselves with the usual vagaries, whims, aberrations, and propensities of human beings or natural bodies;

Second, an able and talented writer will observe, ponder, and record the behavior of these admirable, or despicable, people;

Third, a portion of readers will be entertained and enthralled, or, as the case may be, repelled and disgusted, by the author's description and interpretation of the antics and motivations of his chosen characters; and,

Fourth, another portion of readers, as always, will say that the novel might not be good literature, but that enough action took place to make the story really interesting all the way to the very last page.

What follows now in this volume are some of the personal mementos that have been retained as remembrances of the times when I was absorbed in observing and pondering the behavior of people and recording their antics and motivations. And, of course, during all that time I was mindful that storytelling does not create literature, but that literature can result from storytelling.

I. LOOKING AT

WRITING AS A WRITER

Contrary minded I may be, yet when I think of the arts—though most respectful of their many and various grandeurs—I think not of painting and sculpture and music, but only of the accomplishments of writing. And when I think of writing, I think not of poetry and sonnets—and likewise with all due respect for poets and sonneteers—but my thoughts are of fiction in its two closely related forms of novel and short story.

Just the same, devoted as I am to the art of writing, I do not consider myself as being a member of any cult of literature or a potential candidate for membership—neither of a classical school nor of an angrily complacent coterie.

As the word itself has become defined in my own mind, literature implies a graceful treading along a prescribed course and a slavish conformity to the sensibilities of prejudiced minds. For that reason alone, I have no desire to belong to that community and be obligated to abide by its rules and regulations, because I am not quiet-spoken and I do not have a velvet touch. I behave like a heavy-handed boilermaker in the literary field. I like to hammer-hammer-hammer and make all the noise I can. The din is not going to produce an euphonious sound, but neither is it going to be a muted dirge of despair.

What I endeavor to be, day by day and year by year, is a storyteller in the written word. And if there is such a thing as the art of storytelling, I must admit a devotion to it. It is with this singular devotion that here I strive, with the use of words and the meanings of words and the ideas of the mind, to communicate with the reader by way of the shortest possible distance and the most meaningful implications that fiction has the ability to convey.

Communication from the writer to the reader through the novel and short story will always mean many things to many people. It can mean historical romance, boy-meets-girl, sadistic perversion, fascinating murder and mystery, a sugar-tit pacifier, or science fiction. However, to me as a writer it can be only one thing, and that is having an interesting story to tell—any story—whether it be humorous, tragic, depressing, or inspiring.

Regardless of what it is called, though, communication through fiction is simply a process of using the most suitable form and language to attract the reader's attention and then managing a story in a way that will hold the reader spellbound to the end. One way to accomplish this is when the writer relates a series of conjunctive events in such a dexterous manner that the reader is not unwilling to be transported to the heights or lowered to the depths. And then, in the end, the able writer will gently return the reader to the solid firm-footed ground of his own reality and familiar surroundings. Other than having been merely entertained or gratified, it is likely that his emotions have been aroused and his senses stimulated. After that, if actually the reader has been lastingly impressed and has had his character fortified or his social vision extended, the communication has been a successful one. It might even be called art.

There are many ways to define fiction as we know it in the present-day world.

My own definition of fiction—and this is solely for my own working purposes—is that it is a realistic story of a make-believe world. In order to tell a believable story, fiction first requires the use of a process of discovery and description of the human spirit in stress and duress, in success and failure, in love and hate. This implies, in my own mind, the creation of imaginary people who are lifelike and recognizable; and, after that, then more than being merely lifelike, they are people who will become in printed words more real than living persons.

Fiction is an art, and a lively one at that. Like art in all of its forms, it must be assumed that fiction is primarily a means of communication. Then, being what it is, there must be a sender and a receiver before any consummation or completion can take place. It is this union, this junction, this spark of contact, that provides the relay between the writer and the reader.

In arriving at this union of the writer and the reader, I have knowingly and purposely ignored the existence of the critic, or, as he is sometimes called, the literary eunuch or procurer of the business.

Nevertheless, the critic's place in literary history is secure. All of us, writer and reader alike, will always be able to recognize him at a glance. He is the person who kicks the author's shins and flails the reader's spirits whenever consummation between them takes place without his active procurement. However, as the world progresses and enlightenment sets in, I am sure the time will come when the critic, if he is going to be able to read anything at all, will have to pay for his own books just like the rest of us.

Now having attempted to short-circuit the critic and give him an electric shock, I would like to list the elements of communication between the writer and the reader.

This is how I would express them:

1) *Conception.* In the beginning this is the birth of the short story or novel in the writer's consciousness, the nurturing of it by his emotions, the rationalization of it by his intellect, and the subsequent labor and delivery of it in the printed word.

2) *Perception.* This is the meeting place on common ground between the writer and the reader, the exhibition gallery, the time and place where author and reader meet in an effort to establish a mutually satisfactory value for the story or book.

3) *Reception.* This is the reader's mind, the ultimate end of communication, and the place where the writer's work is appreciated or depreciated, accepted or rejected, praised or damned. There is no other place of appeal for reconsideration after this.

Such are the bare elements of communication through fiction from beginning to end.

Conception is a laborious period during which a work of fiction is formed and shaped in accord with the personality of the author. Each writer has his own method of nurturing the process, sometimes with external inspiration, sometimes with his own inner spirit, and it follows that I have a method of my own. I would express it like this:

Merely to think about a story to be written was not enough to warrant the writing of it.

There was constant seeing and doing, a finding of the good and evil in people and in all the ways of the world. There was a search for the reasons for guilt and innocence, for the motives of love and hate for the causes of good fortune and lifelong despair. These were years of a compelling urge for motion and movement, to touch and feel the harshness and tenderness of life everywhere. And all the while there was profound meaning to be had in a single harsh word, to be heard in blatant laughter, to be seen in an affectionate glance.

This was a beginning, but there was still more to be done before the vision of a story would appear.

Like an actor rehearsing his part before he can go on stage in front of an audience, there were cues to be learned, lines to be memorized, tones and inflections to be realized. But even with that accomplished, writing was not like speaking from memory. The spoken word had to be transformed into the written word. And then, finally, the people of the story had to be those who were able to come out of life and appear at ease while living in the world of fiction.

This, then, was one way of going about the task of bringing to book in printed words the idea to be expressed, the theme to be persued, and the people and events to be brought to life.

Perception is the testing ground of writing. The writer presents his finished work to the reader with the hope that he has found a kindred spirit, a person who will share and appreciate the feelings and emotions of his image of man. The reader approaches the novel with a skeptical mind, but hopeful that he will be entertained, or will profit by the revelations of character and events, or that he will find a vision of life far beyond his own horizon.

Regardless of all else at this exhibition on the testing ground of the novel, there must be contained in the story a motivation that is authentic and meaningful of human kind. There must be a yearning to love and to despise. There must be a compelling urge to cheer for the ultimate success of a fictional person or to weep over his downfall.

These and many more elements are the everyday bits and pieces of a novel, but all of them are worthless and meaningless unless they are used in such a way by the writer that the reader is awakened in mind and emotions and finds himself concerned and gripped by the fictional character who, in the beginning, was nothing more than a given name, initial, and surname printed on paper, but who, by reason of the writer's ability, has become in the end even more real and lifelike than life itself.

Reception by the reader is the aim and goal of the writer, for without readers there would be no communication between the two.

This is actual barter—swapping a story for a dollar. It is commercialization of talent. It is prostitution of art. But it is also the economics of civilization. A worker in the trade of storytelling requires food for his stomach, and it would be a breach of the peace for him to go without clothing. Yet it does not necessarily follow that all writers practice their profession for the sole purpose of making money. I, for one, practice the trade I have chosen because I have an urge to do so—and I doubt if I could make a passable living in any other field—but I do wish, for the sake of economics, to be paid for my efforts.

The end result of these three elements—conception, perception, and reception—is communication in the same sense that the telephone, the radio, the television, the newspaper is communication.

In the present world of advancing science it would seem that communication in the form of fiction would be more widely spread and universal than it is. Aside from periodic local uprisings of censors in such places as Boston, Detroit, and Philadelphia, there is a most serious threat to the free circulation of fiction.

More and more, nation by nation, writers of fiction are restricted in communication for political purposes, not only with readers in their native countries, but with readers in foreign countries. And even when restriction does not openly exist, there is likelihood of some form of intimidation in the background.

This should be a matter of concern to all who live on this globe of earth. Regardless of what country we live in, and regardless of color, religion, politics, and the race to which we were born, we all are human beings. And the human spirit is universal and is not confined to one chosen nation or race alone.

It would be dangerous to the hard-won tenets of freedom to become so accustomed to restricted communication and imposed limits of expression that they are accepted without protest. As it is in many places today, the writer is able to survive only if he devotes himself to propaganda.

Writers of propaganda are not communicating with their readers, but are having their talents used to serve the purposes of political schemes. If there is such a thing as the art of fiction, it cannot be practiced without the free mind and emotions of the writer.

Those who suffer the consequences in greatest numbers in such countries are the readers. Readers are not only deprived of novels of true creation, but are subjected to enervating propaganda—a scientific nerve gas, a dose of tranquilizing pills that weakens the spirit and falsifies the realities of life.

But this is not the total effect of restricted communication. It also prevents the translation of freely created novels from one language to another—from our country to their country, from their country to ours. No advancement in science should be considered to be an achievement as long as the people of the world are the victims of restricted communication—fed the pap of propaganda and rendered as helpless as brain-washed prisoners—because communication itself, vocal, printed, and electronic, is also a science of the first order.

Progress is with us—scientific progress, that is—but human progress will not be able to get up from its knees everywhere in the world and walk freely until there is universal respect for the human spirit. When that time comes, to all people, to all nations, to all races, then civilization will have justified its existence on this particular globe of earth.

II. HOW TO

LIVE LIKE AN AUTHOR

In this way of beginning, like the most noble of the heroes and heroines of our fiction, let us be honest with ourselves and affirm to the utmost the sincerity of our motives.

As it is with me, and I presume to say it is with you, we have come here because of some compelling necessity, and not because it is of our own choosing.

And, assuming this statement to be acceptable, I think it will be safe to say that each one of us would much rather be at home, where the driving urge of writing impells us, and be at work on that great historical romance, that prize-winning short story, that runaway best-seller.

If anyone is doubtful of this, and does not subscribe wholeheartedly to the theory that only writing itself can produce writing, let him take heed, because he is in danger of becoming merely a spectator of writing.

A spectator of writing is neither a good reader nor a

17

passable writer. He is a critical onlooker who considers himself superior to the wearisome task of serving apprenticeship in the craft of writing, but is ever ready to tell you what is wrong with what everybody else writes. And after that, if he persists, he surely will be doomed to that purgatory where all atoning critics wail and writhe in their agony.

But here we are, as writers and as students of writing, because necessity compels us to gather like this from time to time—here, there, and all across the nation—in order to seek what meager solace we can from our common and mutual misery of authorship—authorship attained or potential or earnestly hoped for by-and-by.

Even if we are wasting time and reveling in a convention, we feel justified in what we are doing.

Not belonging to the brotherhood of writers, and therefore existing in a world apart, our friends and severest critics at home, no matter how earnestly they strive, are not capable of expressing the professional sympathy and loving comiseration we need to sustain us through the long hours and dark nights of our travail. And so we must leave home and loved ones and revel among our own kind in the communal atmosphere of a literary conference.

At a time and place such as this, like a convention of professional mourners, long-faced and sad-eyed in keeping with constant bereavement, we congregate at our wailing wall. Leaning on one another's shoulders, our plaintive cry is heard across the land: If you will listen to my troubles, I'll listen to your troubles, too.

However, regardless of the constant unhappiness and frustration imposed upon us by editors and publishers— and not forgetting uncooperative literary agents—the profession of authorship requires that we do our utmost at all times to maintain the traditional kind of front and visage that readers have come to expect of writers.

For one thing, this means that the mask we wear in

public must show us as having the benign smile and kindly countenance of a good gray poet or the rascally smirk of an introspective novelist. For another thing, a witty remark, quotable but unprintable, must always be in readiness on the tip of the tongue. Then, and as important as any, we must acquire and cultivate some outlandish eccentricity, such as bangs or a crew cut, as the personal trademark of our genius.

If it is true that these attributes are really those that readers have come to expect of writers and demand of them, it may be wise for us to accept the fact and school ourselves to cater to their expectations and demands by serious application of this form of literary salesmanship.

In a financial sense, this kind of salesmanship could be very profitable; and if we are discouraged and disheartened by a meagerness of publicity, it might be good for what ails us. Some readers might even become so respectful and enamored of writers that they would actually go to a bookstore and buy hard-cover copies of our books, instead of waiting several years until they are reprinted in paper covers or made into a motion picture.

If we are going to face the fact that writers should recognize the need to look, talk, and behave in a manner expected of us by readers, perhaps we ought to take advantage of such an opportunity to become rich and famous by living like an author even if we have little or no time left in which to do our writing. If we are lucky, we might be able to get one story or novel written. That would qualify us to pose as an author for the remainder of our lives with no more drudging at the typewriter and no more rejections of our manuscripts from editors and publishers.

But, of course, if luck fails us, we will have the comfort of knowing that it is not absolutely necessary for a writer to be an actual author—he can become a critic and enjoy the privileges of an author by depreciating and belittling the published stories and novels of those who do write them.

Anyway, more and more in this day and age, being a writer who writes is not enough. He must learn to act the part with such genuine sincerity and repetitious gestures that he will surely look like an authentic author when he makes his frequent appearances on television programs and lecture platforms.

As an example of this, let us look at a typical author during a typical day of his life while he is doing his utmost to live like an author. Of course, being typical, this will not be one of his writing days, because there is so little time for that now.

His name is Lively Scribbler, and not by mere chance, either. After considerable thought and some study of contemporary human nature, he dreamed up this name for literary purposes, instead of using the name given him by his mother and father, which was Irving Washington. Now as Lively Scribbler, he is able to live up to the average reader's conception of a typical author by having acquired a modern, up-to-date, attention-getting, literary name.

Even so, Lively Scribbler is seriously thinking of either changing his name again, or perhaps writing under several other names which he will dream up, because he thinks that if he was able to attract attention the first time he changed his name, he ought to be able to attract far more notoriety by using other odd-osunding names. But, for the present, on this typical day of his life, he is Lively Scribbler.

With curtains drawn over the windows so that he cannot be observed by a reader walking along the street, Lively Scribbler is reading his morning mail in the breakfast nook of his home. The nook, of course, is the few square feet of space between the kitchen stove and the sink. Otherwise, he would have to sit on his folding cot and hold his plate on his lap.

The reason for the curtains being drawn is that this is a phase of his life that he is ashamed of, because he is con-

vinced that readers ought to eat in commonplace breakfast nooks and that authors should have breakfast bars
and sit on high stools. And, of course, be waited upon by
a serving girl with the physical descriptions of one of his
daring female characters. Anyway, as soon as Lively
makes some money from his writing, which he has not
yet done—being a typical writer—he is going to knock out
a wall and install a breakfast bar with uncomfortable,
backless, high stools.

It is not necessary to describe Lively Scribbler's physical
appearance and the kind of clothing he wears, because,
as it has been said, he is a typical author, and everyone
these days who watches television or attends lectures
knows what one looks like.

There are several bill-bearing envelopes in the mail,
but Lively sweeps them aside unopened. However, there
is one letter that he rips open as quickly as possible. In
fact, he has been waiting a whole year for this particular
letter and, consequently, he has not been able to write a
single page during that time.

The letter is an arresting one. Lively Scribbler's publisher has written to him in a frank, man-to-man, cold-
blooded manner, saying bluntly that of the 10,000 hard-
cover copies of his novel printed, only a paltry 700 copies
have been sold after one year, and that he, the publisher,
is sick-and-tired of publishing books that readers do not
buy.

Moreover, the publisher says, he is sick-and-tired of
paying storage charges on the unsold stock of books and
that he is going to have them ground into pulp and
dump them on the wastepaper market for whatever the
mess will bring.

A post script to the publisher's letter says that he, Lively
Scribbler, can save himself some money by not sending
a telegram begging him to try to sell the reprint rights to
a paperback publisher, because he is sick-and-tired after

having tried unsuccessfully to sell any kind of rights to anybody for any purpose. More than that, he said, he had been unable to sell the over-stock of books to make shredded paper for packing chinaware and glass tumblers, for stuffing twenty-cent baseballs and thirty-cent teddy bears, for wrapping cast-iron pancake griddles, and so on.

This has been an example of the dark side of the author's day. Fortunately, there is a brighter side as well.

Lively Scribbler rips open another envelope. Here is a letter asking him to endorse a new brand of hair tonic, and offering, in lieu of a fee, to send him a case of hair tonic in payment for an enthusiastic endorsement. The trouble here is that Lively has barely any more hair on his head now than he had the day he was born. Just the same, he will write the endorsement, since no photograph will be used, because the hair tonic advertisement will publicize him as being an author and, hopefully, promote the sale of his next book should he ever write it.

But there is still another letter.

This one contains an urgent request for Lively to deliver a lecture at a meeting of the local literary club, which, it is stressed, is composed of lovers of literature. Unmentioned, of course, is the fact that the original speaker is off somewhere on a prolonged drunk and his wife has wired that she will not be able to get him on his feet in time for the lecture engagement. Anyway, the literary club says that it will not be able to pay Lively a fee for the lecture, but reminds him that the publicity he will receive in the local newspaper will be far more valuable than money.

In addition, the letter continues, many members of the literary club will undoubtedly want him to autograph copies of his recent novel. What the letter failed to say was that probably no one present would have a copy of his book, and that two or three persons would approach him after the lecture and hand him slips of paper and even expect him to use his own pen to sign his name.

If this is typical of the woes of some authors, it is to be hoped that it will not become more typical, because any author's life is already typical enough and woebegone as it is now.

Typical of some other writers, of course, are those who stay at home and write. For the most part, writing writers are inarticulate as public speakers, they have an unhealthy appearance when seen on television, and they are not socially congenial at literary teas and cocktail parties. In fact, they may even be downright rude on certain occasions. However, they too live like authors: obscure, reflective, retiring, hard-working, and intent upon the use of whatever creative talents they may possess.

The workroom of such a dedicated writer is a sanctuary in a noisy, raucous, slam-bang world of money-making and hectic notoriety, and here is where he lives his life unobserved but observing, unpublicized but productive. Here in his everyday work he is freed from the impositions of the outside world and is able to strive to bring forth in living images created by mere words a conception of people and events in such a way that readers are more spellbound and enthralled by his meaningful storytelling, and its implications, than by life itself.

There is an obvious reason why a particular writer is successful and another one is unsuccessful. The reason is that it requires years of diligence to learn the craft of writing, and without craftmanship no art can be achieved no matter how sincere the desire or how noble the purpose. Even a seemingly chaotic composition, when artistically effective, has a positive design to its disorder. And when a writer is able to excel in his art with diligence and talent, he weaves a magic web that ensnares and captures the reader's mind and emotions with all the dexterous skill of a spider trapping a blithly unsuspecting fly.

All who write fiction have a purpose in common. The purpose is to strive to express, each in his own fashion and to the best of his ability, a meaningful concept of some phase of human existence. The concept may be inspiring or depressing, it may be commonplace and uneventful, or exotic and exciting; but, whatever the tempo and however slight or momentous the occasion, the driving aim of the author is to give the reader a memorable impression of life.

This concept is either the author's own, derived from personal experience and observation, or it is the interpretation he gives to another person's life.

What this means, essentially, whether in poetry, fiction, drama, history, biography, or journalism, is that when we write we are relating a story of some person or some thing. The craftsmanship of the telling, and the talent we are able to bring to bear upon it, make the distinction between one writer and another writer. Simplicity of style or the complexity of it will set two writers apart. Introspective content or objective subject matter will be distinctive of two others.

The two broad categories of writing—creative and factual—give all writers alike the opportunity to prove worth, and, like all human struggle and endeavor, it is left to each of them to prove what worthiness they have in their chosen field. The poet has no more reason to scorn the journalist than the journalist has reason to scorn the dramatist. A savory taste to one person can easily be a bitter herb to another.

What is common to all who write is the desire to make the finished work, creative or factual, a magnet that will draw the reader to the writing and hold him so enthralled and entranced that he will eagerly resist all competing entreaties for his time and attention. There is only one way of accomplishing this, and that is to make the written work more interesting than life itself, more compelling than the usual distractions of the world.

The minds and emotions of men—and this is the field the responsible writer respects but will not cater to—are more selective and diverse in tastes that the most ravenous stomach or the most sophisticated gullet.

It is due to his respect for the human mind and emotions that the serious student of writing will suspect and question periodic appearances of new trends and new waves which exalt form over substance. Authentic innovations in writing are not the result of chance discovery or invention; they are the result of arduous, painstaking thought and experiment by writers through decades and centuries of work. In all areas of writing, in order to achieve form, first there must be substance.

In the field of fiction, in particular, the heralding of this ism and that tic is usually proclaimed by those who have failed, due to lack of diligence and talent, to produce readable, meaningful storytelling.

Without the magic of its art, storytelling is like a window without a view, love without recompense.

III. THE VIEW

OM A PLACE OF MANY WINDOWS

It can be said that a society or club or an association is an organization composed of a group of persons with mutual interests who have banded together for a purpose in common. No matter how idealistic the aim, however, and regardless of what the individual members think the purpose or the organization is, the treasurer will always say the aim is to pay your dues promptly.

Some organizations are noble in purpose; others are plainly ignoble. Between extremes there are countless societies, clubs, associations, syndicates and clannish cells that merely provide an excuse to have a meeting place where the gregarious can preserve and improve their herd instincts.

When we speak of a literary society, the definition of it is already well-known and no elaboration is needed, but its purpose is not always apparent and explicit. Without a resolute aim, any society could easily become merely an excuse for a pastime of drinking parties and social chitchat.

There are numerous so-called literary societies or literature appreciation leagues from one end of the country to
the other that are secretly dedicated to beer drinking and
poker playing, and that is naming only two of the minor
vices that find shelter and comfort under a respectable
name. If it is not already common knowledge by now, it
should be made known that not all literary societies are
as high-minded and respectable as the term would imply.
At this particular time, however, it can be assumed that
an organization can exist for serious students of literary
matters and that all else is of secondary value.

But that is not all.

In order to justify our presence in an organization of
noble purpose, or at least have a good excuse for being in
the group, it is necessary to be qualified for membership.
The minimum qualification for membership in any literary
society of serious purpose probably means having the
ability to read and write.

But merely being able to read and write should not be
enough. Once admitted through the inner door, the member of a literary society should want to have a comprehension and an acute understanding of what is being read or
written, declaimed or debated.

And, it should be noted, that without fail, there will be
in any society a few misguided members, not content to
be readers, who will actually want to become writers
themselves; or, if they have a lesser ambition, some may
even want to become critics.

Without a comprehension of reading and writing, and
without a continuing study and contemplation of contemporary life and literature, there can be little judgment
of values; or, at best, there can be only a pitiful and misguided conception of people and the way of life. And if
we fail to acquire such understanding, it would be better
for all concerned if we removed ourselves from our literary

society and renounced the pretense of having literate minds. There will always be others who are eager and better qualified to take our place.

There are many simple tests to determine if one has a literate mind. One test is to ask ourselves if the vision we have is capable of letting us see in all directions of the compass as one would from a house of many windows. This implies, of course, that a person will not shut his eyes to the opinions, loyalties, beliefs, feelings, and welfare of other persons. If one should fail this test, he has surely become the victim of prejudice, bigotry, selfishness, inhumanity, and intolerance.

There is little distinction and perhaps none at all, in this appraisal of the literate mind, between a reader and a writer, and certainly there is no superiority whatsoever. Reader or writer, whichever it falls our lot to be, we still must be able to respect the view we see from any place of many windows and not shut our eyes to sights unseen.

The practice of this principle may well lead to violent argument and furious controversy, and it might even lead to a bitterness in social and political life, but even that is better than deliberately blinding ourselves to the facts of life and ignoring the rights of an inquiring mind.

When we speak of reading and writing, we are talking basically about books and authors. All books, such being the product of the human mind and an individual personality, reveal the talent and the genius of the author. Or, as it may be, and often is, the emotional disturbance and mental insincerity of the author is made plain for all to see.

The discerning reader will always look carefully at the book in hand to determine by his own judgment if the author is sincere and responsible, or if he is dishonest and irresponsible.

No one should let himself be misled into thinking that because a book is a book it is above reproach and cannot be thrown into the nearest trash basket. Tainted food and contaminated water can be detected by taste and source. For the same reason, a book should be sampled before being discarded; otherwise, judgment of the author is by hearsay, and not, as it ought to be, by discrimination.

There are numerous writers on every hand whose stock-in-trade is sensationalism and shock—a noxious stew of aberration, crudity, and vulgarity—and they are capable of supplying the commodity in unlimited quantities. And, as most persons know, there are readers who can find satisfaction only in gross sensationalism. But, just as any product is subject to supply and demand, the source would dry up and no market would exist if readers were as discriminating as they are capable of being.

The reading of books, fortunately, is a matter of personal choice, just as much so as is a taste in food and the selection of clothing, and no one should be entitled to have the absolute right to decide what another person should or should not read. Without this freedom of choice, the view from our windows would become limited and restricted and our wide horizon would be lost from sight.

Personally, I would not hesitate to say that any book is worth reading by a person of literate mind—no matter if it is moral or immoral, sacred or profane—because only by reading what has been written can a judgment of values be formed. Contrasts are necessary before there can be intelligent judgment. The literate mind rejects the bad and accepts the good; it is the untrained mind that is susceptible to harmful influence. What we do not know may not hurt us, but it is what we do know that educates us. This is how the world before us and how now we ourselves come by experience, and experience is still an inspiring teacher.

If a person prefers to eat raw carrots instead of marinated rattlesnake, or if he wants to wear Berumda shorts instead of legging himself in Ivy League trousers, he might be looked upon as being odd or eccentric, but at least he made the choice by his own free will and did not submerge his personality by eating corn flakes and wearing a pair of old army pants just because his neighbor does.

In these latter years of life I have come to be more of a writer than a reader—and I think I have earned this respite after having been a youthful book reviewer for five years. In order that there will be no misunderstanding or misconception, I want it to be known that I am glad I had the opportunity and good fortune to be a book reviewer, and equally glad that I had the foresight to resist the temptation to become a critic.

No doubt there is a place somewhere for critics, and I suspect it is a place of eternal torment and retribution. There are many definitions of a critic, but I would like to describe him in my own way. To me, a critic is like the lazy sparrow who moved into a ready-made crow's nest in the top of a tall tree and then squawked and complained about the nest because it was too big for a snug fit and too high above the ground for an easygoing flight.

Anyway, the writing of fiction is my profession, and it is possible that I have learned the practice of it to some degree during all these years. Perhaps I could even think that I learned enough about the profession to be able to offer some advice to anyone who says he wants to be a writer. At the present time I do not know anyone who is lacking in that desire.

The kindest advice I can offer is easily expressed in one word. No! And I think it is worth repeating. No!

Being a writer is devastating drudgery and misery. It is not a self-supporting trade or profession. It is a health-wrecking occupation. It is a craft that defies perfection. Family and friends will secretly pity you. You will acquire a tendency to make excuses at every opportunity for failure and unhappiness in your life. You will always look and act like one of the unemployed.

There are dozens of other trades and professions in life

that are eager and ready to bestow happiness and wealth upon you, and certainly with more ease and plenitude than authorship.

As proof of this, take a good look at the people in any typical American community. More often than not this is what will be found:

A doctor has acquired most of the valuable real estate within the radius of his practice. A storekeeper feeds and clothes his family better than anyone else because he can buy at wholesale. The banker lives in the largest house in town. The automobile salesman always rides in the latest model car. The lawyer takes a longer and more expensive vacation than anyone else. The bus driver is permitted to ride free on his days off. A fireman, day or night, goes to all the spectacular fires. A policeman always marries the winner of a beauty contest.

Writers have never had the good fortune to receive such rewards as these in the past, and they are not likely to, either—present or future.

Even so, there are some persons who are not easily discouraged and disheartened by the inevitable prospect of dire poverty, ill-health, and mental disorders. But, in spite of this, the urge and desire to be a writer will prevail. Such persons as these are indeed fortunate, because they have convinced themselves in the beginning that determination is capable of being a stronger and more lasting force than discouragement.

While it is no guarantee of success, determination does demonstrate a willingness to devote, as a doctor or lawyer or engineer has done, ten years to study and apprenticeship in order to fit yourself for the profession of your choice. What happens after that will be your own life story.

Finally, those determined souls who seek to make authorship a career would do well to keep two thoughts foremost in mind.

The first of these is that luck—good luck—is usually a writer's best friend.

The second is that the more windows a writer has in his house, and the more use he makes of them, the more he will be able to see in the world beyond.

IV. WITH

EYES WIDE OPEN

Something that has always been beyond my knowing is why it is that a writer, an author, a fictioneer of stories and novels is so often called upon to entertain or instruct or even leisurely pass the time of day with a large gathering of hopeful people who expect the impossible. This characteristic American expectation is bound to end in disappointment and disillusionment sooner or later, and this is as good a time as any to get it over with.

If it is not already a well-known fact, it should become evident in no time at all that a novelist is in a sad state when he has no characters to manipulate and no plot to unfold. Perhaps he has a captive audience—which always means a potentially restive audience—but what is lacking is a story to tell. And a novelist without a story to tell is a pathetic creature just as frustrated as a rooster with nothing to crow about.

A wise storyteller would much rather have five hundred sheets of blank paper to stare at and contemplate. In that case, at least he would have somewhat of a chance to dream and perhaps produce on paper something humorous or tragic or inspirational that he could crow over.

However, it is by now a well-known fact that storytellers can be just as gregarious by nature as any rooster can be. All of us who have known our grandfathers can recall the humorous episodes and wild-eyed yarns and hair-raising tales they told us in our youth. Those were the times when spoken storytelling was a real art, and enthralling humor and fanciful embellishments its criterion.

In those long ago days in the country store and at household auctions and around the railroad station, storytelling had to be spellbinding and belly-laughing in order to capture and hold the attention of an audience.

What happened to the postmaster's cow when she got her horns entangled in the merry widow's clothesline, and what the comely widow said to the cow from her downstairs window—well, what was related in forthright language, without reference to the dictionary of synonyms and the syntax of grammar, is still too indelicate to be used in the jargon of psychology, psychopathology, and psychiatry.

Then there was the tale about how the judge trained his guinea hens to start a noisy cackling if somebody struck a match or turned on a flashlight in his chicken house at night, and how his own brother was caught with five frying size pullets in a feed sack—well, it took a good half-hour to tell about that incident with all its fanciful garnish, but it was a tale never to be forgotten. The success of such embellished storytelling was measured by the delighted whoops of the audience and the size of the crowd that had gathered.

Nowadays, the profession of storytelling is a lonely one. It is performed in solitude by a faceless person in an isolated room with little more than a typewriter and paper and a wastebasket. The only opportunity a writer has these days to indulge his gregarious nature is when he is invited to a cocktail party or asked to make a speech in public, being out of practice in the social graces, more often than not he makes an unenviable spectacle of himself on those occasions. Otherwise, the writer sits in his room, typing out his words, and is as far removed from his readers as an incubator chick is from the mother hen—or the rooster.

As the result of this isolation, when a story has been finished and appears in print, the author will be able to read what a critic or reviewer says about his work, but he has no way of knowing what a reader thinks of it. All he can do it to take a deep breath, go back to the confines of his room, begin writing another story, and hope for the best.

It may seem from this that I, as a writer, am unhappy with my lot in life. But that is not so. And the reason I am not unhappy is because I was fortunate enough to learn early and long ago that authorship is not a profession that either creates or tolerates happiness in a human being.

Consequently, I am resigned to my fate, and I know what that fate is to be. As has been in the past, the future will be a zombi-like existence—slightly numb on the inside and quivering on the outside with frazzled nerve-ends. I do not know of any other craft or profession that can promise such sensations and never fail to provide them in abundance.

Everybody has a story to tell, or thinks he has, and, given the slightest encouragement, the next-door-neighbor will tell you his life story without end. In fact, once started, he will be so long-winded and become so enthusiastic that you will not have a chance to tell him your life story. When two such persons get together, it is a futile and exasperating and painful experience. At such times, if you listen closely, you can hear the snapping of taut muscles and the sizzling of frayed nerves.

Nobody wants to listen to another person's life story.

What everybody wants to do is tell his own. It is my theory that that is exactly why and how printing and book publishing originated: It was the only way to give the other person a chance to relate his own story without interruption, and without having to endure the ordeal of listening to somebody else's dull personal history.

Now and then it happens that a person has more than one story to tell. If such a person is willing to serve a long and arduous apprenticeship in the craft of writing, and if he can discover a way to engage the interest of readers, and if he has the talent to do all this better than anybody else—he has a chance to become a professional storyteller and novelist. Even so, there is no assurance of critical success in the profession; there is no guarantee that money will flutter into his lap like the autumn leaves on a windy day in November.

There are many more one-book authors in the world than there are leaves in a whole forest. It is the two-book author who has somewhat of an even chance to become an old pro in the trade.

It is interesting to observe what usually happens when an author succeeds in climbing over that two-book hump. Should he become famous, readers and bystanders who have neither seen nor heard of him before will expect him to appear in public with the ready wit of a nightclub comedian, the roguery of an international playboy, and the glamor of a hard-riding, gun-shooting, accident-prone television actor. Of course he has none of these qualities. After all, he is just a guy.

What every author has to learn sooner or later is that he does not have the superhuman ability to write a three-hundred-page novel and engage in public speech-making at the same time. And aside from that, it is doubtful if there is a writer who could stand up in public and speak a complete grammatical sentence without stumbling and bumbling over some of the words he can readily spell but has never learned to pronounce properly. And because they are sensitive about this shortcoming, that is why there are so few authors traveling around the country these days and appearing on public lecture platforms.

The wise and intelligent authors are safe at home where they belong. And if a writer at home cannot get started on his next novel, or if he is already stuck in the middle of it and is waiting for the proper mood to invigorate his emotions, it is unlikely that he will feel lonely and completely isolated from the rest of the world. He can always while away the time by composing limericks about the bow-legged girl from Winnipeg and the farmer's daughter from Peewee Creek.

If it should be necessary for financial reasons, or to honor cultural obligations, for an author to make an appearance in public, he should not necessarily be obliged to make a speech. An author should be permitted to choose his own method of exhibiting himself so that his personality traits will not be warped and scarred by spasms of stage-fright, tongue-tieing, stuttering, mumbling, and associated tremors. I would not presume to speak for other authors, because they are entitled to their own peculiarities, but in my own case, and in lieu of what I am doing now, I would much rather be bouncing a basketball or playing ping-pong, and I would smile while I did it, too.

But even for the good of so-called cultural and educational purposes, readers and other curiosity seekers should not expect to see a great author in person. With few exceptions, writers never become great authors until they are dead and gone, and their works scattered in the public domain—the graveyard of all writers.

There is good reason for the existence of this public domain graveyard. Publishers of books, who are the ones who advertise and promote the sale of reading matter, take great pride in printing and selling the works of dead great authors. In doing so, they eliminate all haggling and wrangling with live authors in the matter of contracts, options, reversion of rights, division of reprint earnings, and windfalls from motion picture sales. As it is, no money has to be divided when the works of a dead great author go into the public domain.

There are volumes upon volumes of books by great authors long dead in every classroom, public library, and bookstore in the country. And no doubt in almost every home and split-level house there are a number of books in this category. Everybody is assured by publishers and booksellers that these are great books by great authors, and that nobody can consider himself well-read, cultured, status-conscious, and socially acceptable until he has bought the public-domain products of the printing presses.

You can read every play that Shakespeare ever wrote, and there is no royalty involved. You can load your book shelves with all the novels of Tolstoy, Dumas, and Dickens, and there is no royalty payable to anybody. You can read the story of Little Red Riding-Hood—if you have no qualms about not paying the author's royalty for the privilege. It may be that it is for this reason alone that so many copies of the Memoirs of Casanova, the Decameron of Boccaccio, and the Dialogues of Plato are printed and sold every year.

Few living authors, however, are embittered by this royalty-free competition from dead great authors. There is so much to write about in this day and age, so many stories to tell, and so many novels to create that there is no time to mope over this injustice.

Maybe it was Benjamin Franklin who started all this trouble with his printing press, but he should not be judged too harshly. It is enough to know that Benjamin Franklin's own writings are now in the public domain and royalty-free. Anyway, novels are being written now that are great in their own right, even if the author is still alive and can demand and collect royalty. However, it is

likely that these same books will become even more great
after the author passes away and his copyright expires and
he becomes just another cadaver in the public domain.

Readers and students of writing are not to be blamed
for having no real concern about this technical shop talk
having to do with royalties and publishing. Their interest
is in reading for entertainment, or education, and to find
a personal perspective of contemporary life. In order to
find an authentic and acceptable perspective, it is necessary to read contemporary fiction.

In defining contemporary fiction—which is fiction written about and read in the time in which we live—the
reader should make the meaning of the definition clear to
himself in the beginning, for otherwise he takes the risk
of floundering in a swamp of meaningless verbiage. I
would suggest that the ideals of contemporary fiction
should include broadness of vision, depth of perception,
and the artful creation of people and things. When these
qualities are integrated and welded, the resulting novel
can be more meaningful and realistic than life itself. If
this were not so, there would be no purpose in writing and
reading contemporary fiction; the daily newspaper would
be more entertaining and informative.

All fiction does not pretend to come within miles of these
three ideals, and a reader without some standard of judgment easily becomes the victim of the unscrupulous publisher and the avaricious bookseller. On bookstands all
around us is to be found the crude, the vulgar, the sensational, the perverse, and the perverted—all of which has
been planned and designed to appeal to the untrained
mind.

II

It is the untrained mind, either that of a youth or an
adult, which does not have the ability, due to lack of

guidance or to arrested education, to choose and eliminate and make a distinction between the true and the false, between the good and the bad. There is often a narrow shade of difference between these extremes, but the trained mind is capable of finding the distinction.

If a young boy or girl does not acquire this ability to seek the best instead of the worst, it is because parents and teachers have failed in their obligations. If the ability is lacking in an adult, it is too late for anything except an attitude of pity, because he has only himself to blame for not seeking better perception.

The display of a lurid-cover and sensation-title books for sale, which was obviously written and published to appeal to immature emotions and perverted mentality, always brings forth the controversial subject of censorship. Whether it is desirable or not desirable in a free world with a free press, there has always been censorship in the past and there will surely be continuing censorship in the future.

The banning of books is as perennial as the leafage of an oak tree on a hilltop in springtime and the blooming of buttercups in a meadow in summer. Somebody—somewhere right now—feeling morally or politically outraged by a book he has read, will become a self-appointed do-gooder and attempt to have it banned tomorrow.

Censorship exists in all countries where books are written and published, and it is the nature of censorship to vary in intensity from one era to the next, from one nation to another nation according to its social ideals and political purposes. In this connection, it should be remembered that in the beginning a censor was an official Roman tax appraiser and census taker who unofficially took it upon himself to chide and scold people about their immoral conduct while he was counting heads and assessing taxes. He was the first politician of record who also wanted to be a do-gooder, and the tradition has been maintained to this day.

There are three principal causes for censorship at the present time. One of these is for political reasons. Another is for religious reasons. The other is for moral reasons. We are well acquainted, let us say, with the purposes and usages of political propaganda and religious dogma, and there is no reason to speak of those now. The really difficult matter is to decide whether censorship for moral reasons is desirable and beneficial. This is asking where does censorship begin and where does it end, and who is going to be the censor.

If every person had the privilege and the legal right to ban a book, it is a theoretical possibility that no books would exist today. Somebody would surely be offended by some word he found in the dictionary or by some passage he read in the Bible or in the Koran or in the Communist Manifesto.

The customs and mores of society in a free world have always been dictated by people in common as being acceptable or not acceptable. These customs and mores are created by people as a whole and are not the creations of one man or a committee of men. In the end, these customs in turn establish what is moral and what is immoral.

There are many examples of how these social customs come to be established. A style of clothing is acceptable in a particular era, but the same style is not acceptable in a different era. The practice of nudism is permitted under certain conditions, but it is not permitted by custom and law under different conditions. In the history of the English language, certain words became vulgar and obscene in meaning, and they were banished from ordinary usage; the same words reappeared at a later time and again became acceptable by custom. This is the see-saw of social customs and mores.

The meaning of this, I think, is that the people themselves, individually and jointly, should have the right to select and reject, and, as citizens of a country not ruled by absolute monarchy or political dictatorship, they should have the privilege of, and the responsibility for, conducting themselves in accord with the prevailing customs of the country. In other words, let every man be his own censor. This concept of censorship, if it were established, might be the cause of a lot of people finding themselves in jail, but that is one of the customs of the country, too.

After all that has been said here and elsewhere, censorship and the resulting banning of books is still an unresolved and controversial matter, and it is certain to remain so during our lives.

III

In the meanwhile, there is much to be said about the reading of books that remain accessible and are in good standing and are not tainted at present by the labels of propaganda, irreverence, and obscenity.

A taste in reading is acquired by appreciation and discernment. It should be as personal as the selection of a dress or a suit of clothes, and as intimate as the use of a toothbrush. This means that the book should be suitable and fitting, and should conform to the interest and personality of the reader.

It is a dreary chore, and an unrewarding one, to have to read a certain book just because it is said by somebody else to be fashionable to do so. And it is just as much of a dreary chore to feel obligated to read a book that was selected as the book-of-the-hour by somebody who knows nothing of your interests in life and cares less about your personal taste in reading. This kind of forced reading is more harmful and demoralizing to an individual's character and personality than the most recently banned book could ever be. Forced reading takes away the joy of discovery and stifles the adventures of the mind. Forced reading is an iniquitous tranquilizer of the spirit.

A book should awaken and invigorate the mind and

emotions as it reveals life as others live it. And a book that has this quality is not necessarily ponderous and a labor to read—it can be entertaining and a joy to read. But any book should be a window to the world around us—sometimes drab, sometimes wondrous. It is through that window which we can see with eyes wide open a view we have never observed before, and which is as meaningful and immediate and realistic as our own daily life.

There are so many books in existence, so many surrounding us in libraries and bookshops, and still more and more are being written and published every day. A person has to be cautious nowadays before he pays five or six dollars, or even fifty cents, for a book. He has to be aware of what he is seeking, and accept no substitute, or his money can easily be wasted on a piece of shoddy merchandise.

What is now the most important step of all is learning how to select a book—how to reject the inferior and choose the superior. This is not easy, and one must be alert. Even critics who are paid to select and evaluate books as they are published are frequently erratic in judgment and irrational in their recommendations. And of course critics and reviewers are not always impartial—they have prejudice in favor of and prejudice against certain authors just as readers do.

Looking at the portrait of the author on the cover of the book is no help, either; even though the picture has been retouched to give him a he-man appearance, there is something about his looks that convinces you that he could not even change a flat tire. A lady novelist with bedroom eyes proves only that a woman can be beautiful. A writer with a beard proves only that whiskers will grow bushy if a man does not shave.

There are standard brands of books to be bought with eyes shut tight, and without forethought whatsoever. These books are as standardized as a favorite brand of cigarettes, and as unvarying as the kind of coffee and gasoline and toothpaste you habitually buy. But there is no discovery to be made. There is no exciting search for the new. There is no chance to find something better. There is none of the elation of finding yourself face to face with a burgeoning talent.

There is only one way left. Do it yourself. Select your own reading. And do not be afraid of trial-and-error. It will be a rewarding experience, and a memorable one.

But take care. Do not become too proficient. Otherwise, there is the danger of a person becoming so proficient that he might be tempted to go into the business of selecting books for other people to read.

V. WORDSMANSHIP —

THE THEORY, PRACTICE, AND REWARDS OF—

A writer is a person whose calling is that of putting on paper one word after another until he has revealed a fact, proposed an idea, or told a story in an able manner.

This is such a simple definition of wordsmanship that a great number of persons of all callings could easily be led astray and come to believe that they, too, could become qualified and proficient reporters, essayists, or storytellers.

However, before going off to dreamland and reclining on its downy pillows, every person with such ambitions should put himself to the severely realistic test that every writer must face sooner or later. And here follows the test which will be marked plus or minus—and which will result in success or failure:

Do the majority of readers, and you yourself, feel that the composition or exposition is informative, or instructive, or inspiring, or entertaining?

If the answer is affirmative, the writer has a chance to

survive if he has the ability to compete with a hundred thousand others who have reached the same conclusion. If the answer is negative, there is always the remote chance that he is an unappreciated genius.

Regardless of the result of the test, however, no one writer can be all things to all readers. First there has to be a selected specialization in the field of writing. Then each writer must prove in his work that he brings some quality of expression to the reader—whether as reporter, essayist, historian, poet, or storyteller. The quality of expression will vary with the personality, experience, and talent of the individual. And for that reason some writing will be dull and plodding and commonplace, even if acceptable as information; other writing will be vivid and exciting, and sought after for inspiration and entertainment. All in all, whether dull or exciting, the limitations of a writer's talent, and the use he makes of it, will be his only handicap.

II

There are so many fields and branches and byways of writing that only a large group of specialists and experts could possibly encompass the whole sprawling world of wordsmanship. It would take a great number of such qualified persons to be able to offer practical advice and present gems of experience to the aspiring student of writing, and, in particular, to the would-be reporter or storyteller. For example, the field of journalism, and the newspaper in particular, is composed of many departments and categories. Those who are familiar with newspapers will be able to recognize some of the following categories of journalists:

1) *The Editorial Writer*

It is generally believed by the reading public that this anonymous behind-the-scenes personality is invariably high-minded and morally incorruptible; that he is a sincere and dedicated day-and-night watchdog over the political shenanigans at city hall and the governor's office; and that he is the mortal enemy of pinball machine operators and horserace bookies. The principal reason why the editorial writer has become regarded with such awe and esteem is because in the printed word he has never been known to reveal any animosity toward dogs, motherhood, and civic luncheon clubs. What is not known about him, however, is that he never fails to check with the business office and double check with the advertising department before writing an editorial on such controversial subjects as The Necessity For Installing More Parking Meters, Why Should Cats Be Exempt From Taxation?, and The Poisoning Of Pigeons For Civic Betterment.

2) *The Think-Piece Pundit, or Political Analyst*

Everybody agrees that he is a fearless feature writer and the master of tomorrow's fate. He wears a frown of deep thought and appears to be on the verge of challenging destiny to contradict him. Once a week he berates the president's wife for being the cause of the low income of dog breeders and chicken raisers. It goes without saying that he has important political connections at the sttae capitol and ready access to inside-city-hall information. In his writing he is always persuasive enough to make the reader believe that he knows the exact girth of the Princess of Mumbo-Mumble, the ultimate end of Judge Crater, and the undisclosable-in-print reason why the mayor is frantically opposed to a new issue of sewer bonds.

3) *The All-Purpose Propagandist*

From time to time, as the occasion arises, readers of large-circulation newspapers get a taste of the honeyed words of this invaluable staff writer. He is a master of insidious propaganda for special interests—that is, the important space-buyers of advertising. This is the writer who can justify, for example, the cutting down of all the shade trees on the residential streets of the city and make the vandalism sound like civic progress, when actually, as everybody knows, the electric light company would otherwise have to go to great expense to put their power lines underground.

4) *The Roving Correspondent*

Fellow staff members have censorable names for this newspaperman, the mildest of which is likewise unprintable. He can otherwise be described as usually being a fast-thinking reporter who married the owner's daughter. Since attaining his elevated position, he is never available for routine assignments, such as writing the obituary column or taking the police beat. Instead, his dispatches come from far-away places. This is because he and his wife are always attending social events in Washington, going to the opening of new plays in New York, and taking winter cruises to Jamaica and Tahiti.

5) *The Name-Dropping Columnist*

He knows everything that goes on except what is said behind his back by fellow journalists. This man-about-town is always the best-dressed member of the newspaper staff, he has a private office and unlisted phone and leg man of his own, and he never has to pay restaurant and night club chits. And he has no fear of being fired, either, because he has a non-cancellation clause in his five-year contract. Although he does not know the first names of other reporters and is rarely seen at the office except on pay-day, he is in constant demand as master of ceremonies at fashion shows, charity auctions, and beauty contests.

6) *The Party-Hopper Society Reporter*

Every woman reader of the newspaper is envious of the glamorous life of this social chit-chat personality and her first-name acquaintanceship with the elite of society. Readers are convinced that all the better dress shops in town beg her to select all the clothes and accessories she wants at half-price so she will display them at fashionable teas, receptions, lunches, cocktail parties, and weddings. The truth is, however, that she is far from being pleased with her bachelor-girl life and constantly yearns for a home and babies. Every night after work she looks at herself in the mirror as long as she can endure the sight of her plain looks, and then throws herself on the bed and cries herself to sleep. She has never been engaged, she had not had a date in ten years, and it has been a long time since she first began to look over-forty.

7) *The Art and Culture Expert*

Here is a journalist who stands out in any crowd—and especially in a newspaper city room. He is all tweeds and scraggly beard, and a bachelor by quirk of nature. As is to be expected, he is addicted to a vocabulary gleaned from a thesaurus to which only he is privy. Whenever the editor tells him to sharpen and simplify his words so readers can understand what he is saying, he will swallow his pride and grit his teeth while describing a painting or sculpture as being disgustingly gutty.

8) *The Sob-Sister Color Writer*

In this day and age it is not surprising that so many large-circulation newspapers employ an accomplished tear-jerker reporter as a matter of policy—business policy, that is. Hard-nosed thinking in the business department proved long ago by chart and graph that tear-jerking is a better means of building circulation than humor, and frequently even more widely appealing to subscribers than comic strips. And in order to render a public service, the same hard-nosed business managers employed a psychologist to assure readers that an emotional release of their tears would be beneficial to their psyche. In this highly specialized field of journalism, however, it should be remembered that only a practiced and authentic sob-sister, male or female, can successfully wring the heart of the reader in telling of the sad plight of abandoned puppies and kittens, the sorrows of an evicted grandmother, the hysteria of a runaway bride on her wedding night, and the penitence of a blonde gun moll.

9) *The Book Reviewer*

He was once a newspaperman himself, but the editor was a kind-hearted man at times and, instead of handing him terminal salary, presenting him with a ten-dollar watch, and putting him on the street, another place was found for him on the payroll. Now the ex-newspaperman has a daily column or Sunday page, and long ago elevated himself from the job of book reviewing to the position of literary critic. Once he tried his hand at writing a novel because it looked so easy for a man with his superior knowledge of literature, but soon found out that it was more in keeping with his particular talent to criticize somebody else's book than it was to write one himself.

10) *The Reporter*

The authentic newsman writes on any newsworthy topic and does not expect to have a by-line. He is indispensable and irreplaceable. Without him there would be no newspaper.

III

Storytelling, which is the basic element of fiction writing, has long been accepted as bein a respectable component of wordsmanship. Before it became a respectable occupation, however, there was the time when storytelling had the reputation of being merely an excuse for recounting shady tales by word of mouth because they were too raucous and indelicate for print. The early storytellers were the founders of the school of thought which maintained that only the oral method of telling a story could convey the authentic mirth and subtle nuances of a truly humorous tale—or belly-laugh, as it was called by the uninhibited patrons of the art. In those days such tales mysteriously came into existence deep in the country at the crossroad store and were then artfully embellished to perfection. Freeway by-passes and television comedians brought an end to that great American institution now known in history as country-store humor.

Nowadays storytelling saturates the pages of mountainous stacks of magazines and books, sometimes with elegance and sometimes without propriety, but always with an attempt to recapture in type-and-ink some of the spirit and excitement of a bygone art. There is so much rush and hurry by editors and publishers for immediate publication that a newly created story has no opportunity to be embellished and perfected by the craftsmen of the word-of-mouth guild before appearing in print. As a result, editors and publishers, being as eager as they are to fill and fatten their pages, it is not surprising that the same story often appears simultaneously in half-a-dozen magazines and books—but of course with a careful changing of characters and places, and under the names and pseudonyms of different authors.

It must be accepted, regardless of our feeling for the past, that there is little time in contemporary life for leisurely spoken storytelling, and, besides, the teller of tales received no money for his oral story no matter how well he had perfected and embellished it. The author of the written story, in this age of social security and income taxes, looks to be paid for his fiction. And due to the rumor that some authors actually make a living from their work, it is not surprising that so many persons nowadays have ambitions to be writers.

Since each individual fiction writer is presenting his own personality and talent, categories for them would be endless and tiresome. However, the following are surely representative:

1) *The Writer of the So-Called True Story*

To begin with, there is no such thing as a fictional true story. If the story were actually true, and had already taken place, it would be a fact, and the result would be a recital or record of an event as it had happened. A truly fictional story is an imagined incident or episode, or a closely related series of them, which might have taken place but did not, and which the reader is persuaded by the talent and artistry of the writer to accept as an actual event of the past. Even a fictional story based on actual persons and happenings must rely upon the ability of the author to decide what to add to and what to eliminate from the actual facts. Otherwise, boredom is apt to set in and the story will fail to be acceptable and believable to the reader. This means to say that the author is at his best when he is able to say more by implication than by words themselves.

2) *Everybody Has a Story to Tell*

This fragment taken out of context from American folkways has brought more misery and heartache to men and women, and that includes broken homes and dissolved marriages, than all the hillbilly songs and country music composed since the days of Daniel Boone. If a person without writing ability and talent—and this includes movie actresses, country doctors, taxi drivers, and lonely house-wives—believes he has an interesting life story, the only person qualified to write such a book is a professional biographer or ghost writer. Otherwise, if the novice persists in his delusion, he will almost certainly become the victim of a vanity publisher who will take several hundred dollars of hard-earned savings, and even thousands of dollars, to print a few hundred copies of a book nobody will bother to read—except a few friends and relatives who receive free copies and feel that they are obligated to read it.

3) *The Writer Who Might Have Been*

In almost every clutch of writers there is one who clearly demonstrates an outstanding ability and reveals the necessary talent to write interesting and meaningful fiction. As it often happens, though, especially in this hurry-hurry day and age, the chances are that he will forego the necessary training and ignore the required patience that the profession demands and become impatient for immediate success and rewards. If he is unable to restrain himself and if he fails to recognize the value of apprenticeship—which indicate the lack of self-discipline and self-criticism—he is likely to give up a promising future as a novelist to accept the quick acclaim and fast money always held out as a lure in other fields. For instance, public relations and advertising are honorable professions, too, but they belong to categories other that fiction writing.

4) *The Person Who Is Going to Take Time Off Someday to Write a Novel*

This is a most pleasant daydream for anybody, and it is far less harmful than many of the other popular vices.

The contemplation of it all, which can be indulged in day and night, provides a person with something worthwhile to live for and a rosy future to envision. The good thing about this is that it is something to take place in the future and never at hand. Such a would-be writer never has to face the disillusionment and frustration that would come to him after trying to write the first chapter.

5) *The Desire to Be a Writer Is Not Enough*

If anybody could become a professional author merely by wishful thinking, there would be more writers than readers. And since writers are notorious for not reading one another's short stories and novels, the few remaining readers and book buyers would not be numerous enough to support the publishing business. As a result, whole empires of magazine and book publishing would go bankrupt, and hundreds of editors would be without jobs. Fortunately for readers, editors, and publishers, authorship is an exacting profession, and only the fittest and most competent, and at times the most lucky, can survive. And in order to excel in authorship, a writer must prepare himself with no less study, training, and diligence than a lawyer or physician devotes to preparation for his profession.

6) *The Secret of Becoming an Author*

It is a simple matter for anybody to become the author of dozens of short stories and many novels. Only three qualifications are needed. These three are: desire, determination, and ability. Every person is capable of having the desire, many might be able to acquire the determination, but, as it happens, only a very few will have the ability. Now that the secret has been revealed, it is plain that the same qualifications are necessary for those persons who are considering the possibility of being butchers, bus drivers, or bandits.

7) *The Difference Between an Amateur Writer and a Professional Author*

Here is where the scribblers are separated from the experts. The amateur, or aspiring writer, is inclined by inexperience or ignorance to be mesmerized by the magic of his own wordage and, consequently, rendered incapable of being critical of his own work. More than that, and this is the beginning of the end, he is deluded by pride in being able to accept criticism from reader or editor, even a friendly or helpful one, and becomes blinded by personal resentment if such a person tries to suggest ways to improve the composition. All that needs to be said about the professional author is that he himself will be his severest critic. Some of these professional authors will have the gift of instinctive perception, others will have diligently acquired knowledge and skill. In any case, the professional author searches for flaws and defects with all the ability at his command, he is more critical of his own work than any number of readers and editors can be, and, finally, he revises and rewrites time after time in an effort to brighten his story or novel and bring it as close to perfection as possible.

8) *The School for Realism*

Praise, flattery, and encouragement have a rightful place when earned and deserved by accomplishment, but there is scant room for toleration of such encomiums in the hard-nose world of professional writing. In such a realistic arena, the best possible encouragement is forthright discouragement. This may sound harsh and ruthless and perverse, but the dedicated writer will not accept defeat as long as he has confidence in himself, and discouragement will impel him to strive even harder for success. It is always difficult for any person to be discouraging to another person, and likewise it is not easy for a person to accept discouraging comment and criticism without a feeling of resentment and certainly with any degree of grace. This is a realistic situation, though, and not one to be tampered with and diluted with sentiment. All that needs to be said now is that the writer with faith in his own ability and fortunately blessed with dogged determination will always be inspired to prove to one and all how bright and shining his talent can be.

9) *The Craft of Wordsmanship*

If there ever was a do-it-yourself hobby or enterprise, meaning one for which a person supplies his own do-it-yourself kit, it is the writing of fiction. This is a one-man job. It is as personal and lonely as the act of committing suicide. Schools of writing and professional teachers and proficient critics, and even sympathetic editors and publishers, are helpful as such when they provide a forum for advice and a workshop for trial-and-error. Just the same, no school or instructor can provide a do-it-for-you kit. In the hard-nose craft of professional wordsmanship, it is every man for himself.

10) *How to Be a Successful Writer*

It is easy to propose a question like this, because the answer is such a simple one. In order to become a successful writer, there are only three things to do. First, learn how to survive on wild berries and bird eggs; second, reject all the fine print in a publisher's contract; and, third, write better than anybody else.

When an author has escaped from the tedium of his

typewriter and has some relief from the racking of his brains, he may be offered an opportunity to express himself in spoken words instead of the written ones. When this does happen, it is not surprising that he is inclined to take advantage of the freedom to give vent to his favorite prejudice. Not being a great thinker or philosopher, and certainly not a practiced and cautious orator, he is apt to misspeak himself and make rash judgment while discharging his pent emotions. This, however, is the risk of the spoken word, and all who utter it must assume the consequences of being misunderstood and misjudged.

Not being one myself, fortunately, and not likely to be welcomed into the brotherhood in the future, I can be without reserve or reticence in saying that the poverty of contemporary fiction has been caused by the inept, inert, and inadequate knowledge and experience of the American literary critic. And if I had an invitation to express myself in a more precise manner and granted the privilege to make the charge more chiding and goading, I would certainly do so.

In generations past, the status of this man of letters has been of noble proportions, and upon reader and writer alike was reflected the wisdom and judgment of a superior mind which had been nurtured by worldly experience. But not so the critic of today. Not having had the physical touch and feel of common humanity, he can only resort to brain-picking somebody else's scholarship as a substitute. This is why part of the time he is stampeding with the herd and why the remainder of the time is devoted to the childhood game of follow-the-leader.

This hard look at the present-day literary critic, as he presumptuously insists upon being called, was prompted by a sampling of recent writings by several of the most eminent of the clique. In each instance the critic was reviewing a contemporary American novel. It is almost beyond belief, but, as if acting in concert, each critic ignored the author's attempt to explore and reveal meaning in contemporary American life. Instead, these self-styled pundits expounded at length upon the charge that the author failed to write in the accepted traditions of the great novelists of the past.

The only possible explanation for this state of mind is that today's critics got their learning by rote, and from the same suspect source at that. The term rote is used here in kindness, because to call it a strange coincidence would be too harsh in its implication. Just the same, somebody, somewhere, was the prime source of a postulate on criticism that has been faithfully memorized and slavishly idolized by the current generation of literary critics. It would not be surprising to find that they also look alike and use the same brands of soap, hair tonic, and pep pills.

In contrast, one of the most astute and penetrating commentators on writing I ever knew had been a boilermaker in his younger days, and every sentence he produced had the authentic ring of truth and the ear-jarring sound of experience.

What a misguided literary critic fails to comprehend is that imitation of the past is a deprivation of the present. It is the nature of the novel, as the word itself immediately implies, to describe the new and interpret the present. The novels that were written in what has been called the great tradition were descriptions and interpretations of contemporaneous persons and events, and thereby established traditions of their own by ignoring and not imitating previous traditions. Such traditions of the past should be guides and starting points for today's novelists, and not ends in themselves. Experiment and individuality and a keen awareness of contemporary life will always provide the material and inspiration for more profound novels than the past has ever produced. This concept, and this only, is the one valid tradition worthy of continuation.

It is the nature of the human being to have an absorbing interest in storytelling. Beginning with childhood, when we hear for the first time the exciting tales about bears and foxes and rabbits, there is progressive interest in life around us. Soon our imagination is aroused and activated by the strange sounds in the night and the mysterious creatures that prowl in the darkness. Then year after year as we grow older our vision and experiences expands until the whole world of man comes into view. Then curiosity sets in, and that is when we have a compelling desire to observe the secret as well as the overt behavior of people and to hear their spoken words and to know their intermost thoughts.

Civilization tends to restrict us to our native environs and to deny us the privilege of unlimited adventures and observation. Thus being social and economic prisoners with limited horizons, we become even more curious about the lives of people elsewhere, whether they are actual or imaginary, and we want to know about them in the printed word. In order to satisfy that curiosity, we look to the reporter, the historian, the biographer, and the novelist. All of these writers are storytellers in the true sense of the word.

The reporter, historian, and biographer are concerned solely with the facts and figures of life and are motivated by the desire to record such information accurately and interestingly. Their style of writing and their interpretation of people and events are created by experience and personality.

The novelist and short story writer, like none other, is licensed to do outlandish things with his fiction. He is not obligated by law or custom to prove that such-and-such a thing actually happened or that a particular character ever existed in life. His only limitation is his own imagination. He is permitted to imagine, to invent, and to create persons and happenings as long as they conform to the laws of probability and to ethical customs. He has the privilege to saturate his pages with perfume or with mephitism until our senses are stultified. He can populate his fictional world with men and women who live by mayhem and murder. He can bring all the saints of heaven to stand before our eyes and inspire us with their goodness.

In the use of his license, all the novelist and short story writer has to do to accomplish his fiction is to make his storytelling meaningful and convincing and interesting. And, as always, the superior author implies more than he says in print. Such is the doctrine of wordsmanship.

This summation of writing as art and craft may sound so simple and easy that it would seem that anybody so inclined could become an accomplished writer. However, apparent ease and simplicity of execution may be decidedly deceptive and misleading.

In order to achieve the meaningful and convincing and interesting, a writer must know and understand the nature of man and the motivations of mind and heart.

A writer can acquire this perception and appreciation only by personal experience and observation. No writer could begin to write about human beings if he had never seen one.

VI. FOUNDER'S DAY

AT METHODICAL COLLEGE

It is my understanding that I am the first author to be invited to prepare and read a paper at an assembly of students, faculty, alumni, and the benefactors of Methodical College.

I have a feeling, now that we are face-to-face in this auditorium, that at the conclusion of this address a second precedent will be established. What comes to mind is that the president and board of regents will rule that in the future no more itinerant writers will be permitted to speak on this campus.

Heretofore, as everybody knows, such an honor as this has been traditionally reserved for and bestowed upon the donor of the new gymnasium, or upon a former student who learned how to rig the stock market, or upon the politician with the best prospects of becoming the next governor of the state.

I have been told in confidence by a friendly student,

and I have given him my pledge not to reveal his name, that no such eminent person, due to adverse financial conditions and the uncertain political situation, qualified for the honor this year of inaugurating the celebration of Founder's Day at Methodical College. This certain student left me with the clear impression that I was chosen to be the speaker for the occasion because it has been rumored that I once gave a lecture elsewhere and did not go to court to force payment of the promised fee.

Just the same, this unique privilege and honor calls upon me, as the person prevailed upon to pay his own expenses and ride the midnight bus from Kansas City, to produce and deliver a skillful and sufferable paper that will be strictly in keeping with the well-known conservative traditions of Methodical College.

Furthermore, the invitation implored me not in any way to imply or suggest by word or gesture that students in this place would be a lot better off if they had had the foresight to seek an education elsewhere. I did not realize the full implication of this request until I got off the bus at sunrise this morning and saw the place with my own eyes.

Be that as it may, I do feel the necessity, as a matter of personal honesty, to say in a moment of frankness that I think a higher type of speaker could be obtained in the future if he were at least offered something to eat during his stay at Methodical College and given the opportunity to have access to an outhouse or some other type of toilet facility while he is on the campus. So far, I have already made two trips back to the bus station, and that is a long walk to have to take each time.

Now to the matter at hand.

It seems appropriate, and in keeping with the traditions of Methodical College, to employ the use of personal pronouns on this occasion as an informal means of immediate and intimate communication between you and me. As we all know, the founder of Methodical College, the late Ike Unough, always referred to the institution as M.C., and he himself preferred to be called I.U.

I am sure the much revered I.U. would be very pleased if he knew that you and I were here today dedicating this hour as a memorial to his well-known reactionary principles of education. But for my part, to tell the truth, I think fifteen minutes of this is all I am going to be able to endure. However, when I do leave, it will be with deep sorrow and a heavy heart, because I will be taking with me an unerasable memory of all you students being stuck here throughout your college career and having no chance of being able to escape.

I am accustomed to thinking of myself as me, and I can assure you that when you finish the time you are here to serve, you will find your own real self again. It will come as a pleasant and welcome surprise to graduating students, when they finally enter the outside world after four long years of confinement in Methodical College, to discover that such names as Jack, Charley, and Mushhead are in acceptable and respectable usage in business, professional, and social life.

Needless to say, and I do sympathize with you, it will have been a long and humiliating term of confinement for you to have to grit your teeth and submerge your personality as a member of the team, as a nonentity in the aggregate, and at all times a mere digit in the statistics of Methodical College. Nobody objects to members of the football and basketball teams having numbers on their backs, but why should every student be numbered like a convict?

It has been a full hundred years to this day since individual given names, nicknames, and surnames were prohibited by I.U. at M.C. From the earliest times to the present day, students on this campus have been issued and required to wear numerical identification, and, admittedly, it is an arresting and unique sight to see numbers stamped on blue-and-orange license plates and worn suspended from the neck. This custom, thanks to you-know-who, is still unique in the educational world and is not likely to be imitated by any respectable institution of learning.

At the same time, however, it is understandable that the professors, immersed for fifty or sixty years in traditions of Methodical College, take pardonable pride in wearing as a status symbol oversize orange-on-blue plates low-numbered B.A. 1, M.A. 2, Ph.D. 3, and so on according to tenure of office and the infirmities of age.

But we are speaking too much of the present, and that might lead to unlimited and uninhibited speculation about the future. The purpose of celebrating Founder's Day at Methodical College, and in particular this one-hundredth anniversary year, is to reaffirm our faith in the tried-and-true platitudes of the past in honor of you-know-who and pledge our allegiance to his reactionary concept of higher education.

As everybody is aware, the mere mention of Methodical College instantly brings forth vivid visions of the past. For thousands of former students it will forever be a never to be forgotten place of rangy jack rabbits, rolling tumbleweeds, roaring tornadoes, howling coyotes, pesty gophers, and no juke boxes and pinball machines within a hundred miles. Here, looking like the weathered ruins of abandoned homesteading shacks on the treeless, windswept, gopher-burrowed, grasshopper-infested prairie are clustered these dilapidated lean-to structures untouched by paint or carpenter's tools since they were pegged together a hundred years ago.

Other colleges from one shore of the nation to the other, unhampered by the do-nothing let-it-be traditions established here by that late person previously mentioned, are constantly digging and filling, hammering and sawing, training the ivy and mowing the lawns, modernizing the old and erecting the new. To be honest about it, only Methodical College could possibly take pride in its timeless symbol of creaking floors, leaking roofs, rat droppings, and a poor imitation of Genghis Khan's dig-and-fill sanitary methods.

As every freshman student is well aware when he first sets amazed eyes upon this pile of antiquity, he is instantly struck speechless and usually remains spellbound well into his senior year. By that time he has become so mesmerized by the sound of scampering little feet between the walls that he remains mute for fear of violating the time-encrusted traditions of that fellow who founded the place.

It is true, or so I have heard on the grapevine, that in recent years there has been some audacious grumbling and griping among a certain element of the student body which has no respect whatsoever for the time-honored reactionary traditions so well and firmly established once and for all by what's-his-name. However, these are unconventional times and it is to be expected that there will be a few unoriented and rebellious students at Methodical College who will agitate for revised textbooks and a new generation of frogs and cats in the biology lab.

As it has long been a policy of academic freedom at all other places of learning, a reasonable amount of grumbling and griping should be tolerated at this institution as a means of discharging youthful impulses and excess energy. After all, it is only a sign of general unrest and political rebellion in the outside world today. Eruptions of dissatisfaction on the campus is clearly understandable when it is remembered that students these days are forced to come to Methodical College against their will and better judgment by parents and grandparents who studied the very same dog-eared textbooks and looked at the same tired old frogs in the biology lab fifty and a hundred years ago.

As an example of this grumbling and griping on the campus today, I, myself, during this first and last visit to Methodical College, listened in amazement to the complaints of numerous students that they had no football coach to hang in effigy, no rocks in the geology lab, no car-ports for their convertibles, and no co-eds to panty-raid. It is ridiculous to expect the modern student to acquire an education under such adverse conditions.

To be honest about it, I want to say that I am thankful that I was not tricked or coerced into coming to a place like this to try to get an education. I feel sorry for every student on this campus, because I know you came to Methodical College with the hope and ambition to acquire an education and a badge of knowledge.

My advice is to do everything possible to transfer at once to any other college that will admit a former student from this place, even if you have to start all over again in the freshman class and, undoubtedly, take summer tutoring as well.

In closing, I want to take this opportunity to say that as far as I am concerned you can put a torch to Methodical College and reduce it to ashes on this god-forsaken, gopher-burrowed, grasshopper-infested prairie. The only qualm you could possibly have is feeling sorry for those mice and rats between the walls who will have to get out and find another place to live.

And if you are wondering why this has been such a brief Founder's Day speech—the next bus for Kansas City leaves in ten minutes.

VII. THE

EVENT OF FICTION

In recent times both the readers and makers of fiction have become the victims of a deluding and fallacious definition of storytelling. A reliance upon an outmoded definition of the past, if not revised, will baffle the readers of today and continue to be misleading and deceptive in the future. The reason for the needed revision is that the novel, as an accepted derivative of a word of basic definition, is by nature in constant change. A comparison of typical novels decade by decade during the past hundred years will reveal an uninterrupted and progressive change of style and content.

As the result of such an investigation, it will be found that only a small percentage of novels of the past have been able to survive and bridge the years and to become classics of all time. For the most part, fiction is as temporal and fleeting as the weekly magazine and daily newspaper. And so is its nature to be. Otherwise, fiction would be as standardized and immutable as the paying of utility bills and income tax.

In order to establish a distinction between the enduring and the transitory, a judicious re-defining of what is known as fiction would clarify the meaning and banish many prevailing misconceptions which originated in the folkways of long ago. It is admitted that this would amount to an ambitious undertaking for the most accomplished etymologist and lexicographer; and, also, that it is doubtful of his being successful in dislodging all erroneous definitions and effectively supplanting them with authentic wording.

The fact is that definitions have a way of following ordinary usage and, even if they do not get recorded immediately in the dictionary, they still have no respect for the previously prescribed rules regardless of how earnest such pronouncements were in concept and motive. In effect then, definitions are unruly and lawless, and even those in good usage today are likely to be obsolete or in questionable usage tomorrow.

To find a way to illuminate the authentic meaning of what is known as contemporary fiction, in the absence of an authoritative definition, and to do the next best thing under the circumstances, it would be necessary to know what fiction nowadays actually is and, even more important, to be aware of what it is not. To arrive at that distinction, any current novel of the day, whether good, bad, or merely so-so, would serve as an example for study and contemplation. A choice can be made from any classification: science fiction, historical romance, murder mysteries, erotic shockers, or poetic nonsense.

To go back to the origin and birth of fiction, it can be said that regardless of a multitude of classifications there are only two primary reasons for the existence of novels. One of the reasons is to read them; the other reason is to write them. All ramifications of this, either for the purpose of art and culture, or for trade and commerce, have this common source.

However, as a caution in passing, it should be remembered that merely because a person is capable of reading a story it gives him no ability whatsoever to write one. Wise readers will be spared considerable pain by confining themselves to being patients and leaving the surgical operations for qualified practitioners to perform. In this same connection, it will not be necessary to advise authors to avoid reading. Authors read only their own books, anyway.

Whether humorous or satiric or serious in subject and content, the basic element of fiction is friction—or as it is sometimes called, conflict. Otherwise, when friction or conflict is lacking, nothing out of the ordinary really happens, as a reader would say when putting a partly-read book aside, and the result is a boring and unrewarding rhetorical exercise.

Such a composition without friction, no matter how sincere and idealistic, is nothing more than simple narration without meaningful motive and implication. Since such static narration has neither cause nor effect, it is without purpose and intention. Even at its best as narration and description it is still obviously an imitation, and not a creation, of life. Masterful storytelling of conflicting motivations is always necessary to keep the novel from being a waste of time and money for the reader and an artistic or economic loss to the author.

As all perceptive readers of novels are well aware, fiction is an image created by the imagination and is not a tape-recording or a transcribed inventory of stock on hand. It is a vivid silhouette of people and things constantly in action which is projected upon the mind and perceived by the emotions.

This image on the mind, once it is established, can become so absorbing that all else is excluded from the mind during the reading of the story and a remembrance of it is likely to be long lasting. The mental and emotional re-actions produced by this seemingly real and lifelike image —whether good or bad, inspiring or depressing, entertaining or educational—are those of the reader, but they were primed by the art and artifice of the author.

Once the images have been cast upon the mind, few readers, regardless of intellect or sophistication, are able to stifle or deny emotional feelings and passions. Tears, laughter, excitement, stimulation, inspiration, envy, revulsion, pity, and sympathy can be dredged from the hardest of hearts and brought to the surface by these artful creations. Such images are convincingly real and lifelike.

Being fiction, a story is something that did not actually happen, but something which might have happened. Further, it may never take place in actuality, yet it seems possible for it to occur in the future. Or so the reader is led to believe. The ability of the author to produce this illusion in another person's mind, to state the principle of fiction once more, is the talent of art and the craft of artifice.

Fiction, consequently, is not reality, but the illusion of reality is real and genuine. Even the label of realism or re-alistic or naturalistic placed upon a novel signifies only that it is a modification of the real for the purpose of fiction. When artistically convincing and emotionally moving, fic-tion will always have the magic gift for being able to pro-duce more tears or laughter or contemplative thought than anything in life itself.

At its best—and there is no room here to be concerned with the second-rate and the commonplace—fiction is a deft and magic projection of the imagination beyond all existing limits of reality. Such creation is the making of something that did not previously exist and which there-after becomes a lasting landmark in the eyes of all who behold it.

If an interim definition of fiction has been achieved, there is one certainty about it. When next year's novels appear, the definition will have to be revised once again to prevent it from being misleading and deceptive, because nobody is able to predict the vagaries of fiction.

II

Every person has his own particular reason for reading fiction. One person will say it is an enjoyable diversion; another will say it increases his knowledge of life; and others will say it is a cultural and social privilege or obligation.

Whatever the reason or excuse, the reading of fiction is likely to be an adult reversion to the fantasies of childhood with the hope of reviving the ecstasies of youth. Hopefully, all pain and disappointment and discouragement of the past can be made to vanish like magic, leaving only the pleasurable memories of that carefree time of life.

That was the time in youth when one was intrigued by the stories of the wonders of the world and felt a close affinity with pets and wild animals. This association with the past provides a ready means of escape from the disillusionment and unhappiness of the present and revives the roaming thoughts and exciting escapades of the past. It brings to memory once more the romance of young love and all its glamor and ecstasy and heartache.

But it is not every reader who will admit that he seeks solace in memories of his youth. In particular, the sophisticate feels superior to such human yearnings, or at least he makes a pretense of it, and goes out of his way to insist that his motives are purely cultural and intellectual. Naturally, when there is such a market to be catered to, there will always be novels purposely contrived and written to supply that pap and pablum.

In fact, there are so many types of novels, and such a number of variations easily come to mind, that limitless categories would be required to contain them. Extraordinary time and patience would be needed even to put into proper place the murder and mystery novels and their varieties, the diversities of historical and costume romances, and the mutation of novels of social protest and religious incantation and political propaganda.

To go to another extreme, categories would have to be made for novels about renegade cowboys, escaped convicts, college professors, piano players, ballet dancers, night-club comedians, diabolical doctors, slovenly housewives, whimsical gamekeepers, and so on endlessly. The certainty about all this is that any subject is acceptable and adaptable as long as it is done with masterful storytelling ability.

Somewhere between these extremes is the here-today-gone-tomorrow fiction written to supply an anticipated or hoped for demand. These novels are usually put together in a hectic tempo by threading a grab-bag of words on a string like so many ill-assorted beads. Some of this will be so-called adult or sophisticated fiction, which is essentially an erotic perversion or a substitute for unfulfilled and unattainable desires for the mentally and emotionally retarded. The effect it has is to supply a semblance of abnormality for the neurotic and act as a temporary narcotic for the jaded.

All of this can be classified as technical or mechanical fiction, because it is always obvious that it is a made-to-order imitation of the creative process. It contains contrived plots with easily predictable characters and situations. It contains invented shocks that strive to be more shocking than the shocks in yesterday's counterpart. Obviously, it is a shoddy imitation and paraphase of a fiction previously written and published.

Perfection has by no means yet been realized in fiction,

and the great American novel still remains to be written. This is unlikely to happen until the author achieves absolute objectivity and refrains from influencing characters and situations with the prejudice of his own mind and personality. The handicap of authors in the past has been that they dictated the action and motive of the story with a preconceived notion of what is good and what is bad. Idealistic or sympathetic, it makes no difference; mores and customs have the only authority to make distinctions between the moral and the immoral.

III

The theory of the purpose for reading fiction is a subject of endless and tiresome debate and discussion, and in the end it always remains unresolved and inconclusive. On the other hand, the practice of the writing of fiction is not a matter of opinion and conjecture, and it can be resolved and made conclusive in few words. It is as natural as falling rain for everybody to want to be a writer.

On the daily evidence of pleading letters to authors and editors, it does seem that every human being at some time in his life, if not continuously, has a fervent desire to be a writer. This ubiquitous urge, if not forthrightly scotched, often becomes an obsession of wishful thinking to a feverish degree and is alleviated only when sanity is effectively restored by hard knocks on the head.

Some persons will argue that this universal obsession to write something is motivated by a deep-seated need for self-expression; some will offer the excuse that everybody has an interesting life story to tell; and others will say that writing looks like a quick and easy way to make money. Whatever the reason or excuse, the results are apt to be agonizing disillusionment and disappointment.

Fiction, un-like poetry and painting and flower arranging, is not a suitable or practical repository for self-expression; the recitation of a life story is always more tolerable in a congenial social gathering than it is to read in a book; and it is much easier to become a millionaire real estate speculator than it is to become an author.

A rational person will successfully dose himself with cold pills and colic syrup and headache powders and never once be deluded by thinking he is a physician. Somebody else will go ahead without a demurrer and pay a two-dollar parking fine and never think he is a lawyer. And yet the same persons will be among those who read a story or novel and be utterly convinced that they, too, can easily be authors.

The blame for this, aside from the normal conceit of the ego, lies in the fact that the visual appearance of a story or novel in print, which has been carefully edited and proofread and is without visible signs of laborous effort, looks as easy and effortless to achieve as the gesture of lighting a cigarette on the leeward side of the street on a calm day in June. In blithe ignorance, such a person never realizes that a passable knowledge of grammar, carefree week-end leisure, and an up-dating of one of his grandfather's favorite anecdotes is not the way fiction comes into existence.

The everlasting, drudging practice of writing is the way fiction is produced. Practice, constant practice, and consuming practice, for nobody knows how many years, combined with suitable ability and talent, is the way fiction is created. What it amounts to in the end will determine whether it is readable and publishable. During all this time, no one is a writer until his work appears in print. Even then he is not a professional author until he is paid for his work and supports himself, at least in part, from the monetary proceeds of his writing.

Unless a person is subsidized by fate in some manner, which usually means a willingness to support himself with a menial job, or perhaps being supported by an institution or by the generosity of another person, there is little possibility of his being able to support himself by writing while he learns. This is an economic factor that enables only the fittest and most determined to survive the ordeal of apprenticeship. If the unfit were not eliminated by some process and sent on their way, the world would be cluttered with anguished people wailing and bemoaning in common misery. The fortunate ones are those who have come to realize and be sufficiently convinced that writing as an occupation is not for them and that the humdrum work of the world will be more likely to reward them with happiness and success.

The survivors of these trials and tribulations are the writers who have the proven stamina and talent to compete in the professional world of writing. Step by step they will become, or at least have the best opportunity to be, the eminent storytellers and novelists of next year and thereafter.

If there is any other way to become a writer, it is being kept a well-guarded secret.

IV

Style in writing is the personal possession of an author and the symbol or trademark of his personality. A style itself is a way of writing that results from the application of individuality upon the essence of storytelling. It develops slowly and consciously over a period of time, practiced and revised and improved, and it is not a miraculous flash of inspiration or genius. Even when seemingly fixed and inflexible, style nevertheless must be at all times adaptable and at ease with the content and subject matter of fiction.

Often there is abject failure and agonizing heartbreak among learners of writing who mistakingly think there is a short cut and an easy way to the attainment of an individual style. This unfortunate misconception has led many potentially good writers to early failure and ruin from which they can never recover.

Imitation of another writer who has an established and widely admired style is on the borderline between theft and flattery. If it learns toward theft, it is only a step away from plagiarism; if it inclines toward flattery, even in all sincerity, it can never be as effective and potent as the genuine.

No less unfortunate is the learner of writing who industriously reduces to an outline the content of another author's successful novel. With this in hand, the novice would consider it to be a plot that could not fail and that a clever rewriting or paraphrase would assure duplication of success. The result might even have the appearance of technical or mechanical perfection, but something of importance will be lacking. Without inherent originality and perception, and not infused with the personality of the creator, such an imitation will be a crude infringement and a bogus pretension. Readers and critics are always quick to perceive and disdain the spurious.

There is always the danger that the learning writer, though no fault of his own, will be misled by somebody into thinking that a plot makes a story or novel and that all else is a modish clothing of words on the skeleton. Authors themselves may be reluctant to give away their professional secrets, and many are notorious for avoiding candid replies to prying questions; however, they do know that so-called plots are extracted or derived from novels after the fact and are not invented as a prelude.

Friction or conflict of character and circumstance, to state a theory once again, creates fiction; no amount of plotting, as it is euphemistically called, is a substitute for creation. The plotted novel will always have the glaring earmarks of contrived and crafty and improbable fiction. Such a novel is always, like the taking and use of another person's words and ideas under the guise of research, an embarrassing and telltale revelation of ignominy and just plain stupidity.

VIII. CONTEMPORARY

READING AND WRITING

It took thousands of years in time, supernatural visions of artistic perfection, and a great deal of laborious effort to do it. That is, to foster the evolution of storytelling from the primitive cave drawings of our ancestors to the anthropological musings of a wayward waitress walking the North Beach streets of San Francisco and to the enticing whispers of a respectable nymphomaniac plying the French Quarter alleys of New Orleans. The many examples of contemporary novels are the evidence that zeal and determination have succeeded in making the profession of storytelling a salacious commodity and a commercial success. As time goes on, however, storytelling will surely become a respectable trade or craft.

The authentic history of storytelling has much more than this to reveal, though; it was not the acquisitive instinct for rewards of money alone that inspired this evolution. There is another important phase in history vitally concerned with the progress of storytelling from the earliest times to the present day. This has to do with the cycles of propaganda in fiction for the causes of Zen Buddhism, Moslemism, totenism, Christianity, yoga, polygyny, monogyny, impressionism, expressionism, socialism, communism, war, peace, and, perhaps, community property taxation laws. Thus, the commercialization of sex and sensuality is actually a minor chapter in the history of storytelling.

Even hasty and casual reading of contemporary fiction will reveal the effects of commercialization and propaganda. In all the strive and push to gain fame and money, the most important element of fiction—which is storytelling—has been gradually eroded and frequently eliminated entirely.

On one side of the world, the ruthless commerce of writing, publishing, and selling books too often takes precedence over the art of the creation of fictional persons and the bold expression of enterprising ideas. In some other area of the world, boldness of expression and freedom of creation are limited and often completely eliminated by the necessity to conform to regulated ideas and prescribed propaganda.

The reader in all instances, no matter where he lives on this earth, is not always given the freedom of access to the true authentic spirit of the writer's art. One result is that the work of a talented writer is rejected by a publisher because he considers it to be an uncommercial property and, therefore, of no economic value to his business. Another result is that the same book is censored elsewhere because it is political dynamite.

Fortunately, there is a way out and blessed escape from this morass of commercialism and propaganda wherever it exists. As it tends to happen in times of prohibition and repression, there will always be venturesome bootleggers to peddle novels that reveal true art and the idealism of storytelling. Whether lurking around the corner with a beckoning finger by day or traveling by night with a bulging bookbag, these furtive citizens may not realize it, but they do render a gratifying public service. Even though the clandestine book peddlers have a purpose at hand that may be considered by some persons to be ignoble and unlawful, their actions at least have the outward appearance of being motivated by the theory that the good of society has never been harmed or endangered by freedom of thought and bravery of the human spirit.

The economic law of supply and demand, when left untampered by political manipulation, and which is otherwise well-established by custom, was no doubt formulated in the earliest times when enthralling storytelling was held at a premium and could only be had by barter on the side. In the present day many a book of exceptional merit can be obtained only by cajoling or bribing the bookseller to forget his greeting cards and party-joke novelties long enough to place a special order with the publisher or to make an extensive search for the out-of-print. By the time the book is obtained, it may not have been bootlegged, but the cost of it is certainly an under-the-counter price.

II

The novel is not a material substance; it is reactionless to chemical and physical tests; and it is not even something that can be calibrated, circumscribed, measured, or delineated. Consequently, it is not easy to define or even vaguely describe a thing so changeable and inconstant and variable. And, perhaps for that reason, it certainly is not easy to write it. The contents and proportions of a novel, for the purpose of critical or academic study, may be readily catalogued and analyzed; however, a resulting concoction, like the blending of the ingredients of a recipe for Bombay curry, will always be mutable and unpredictable and, more often than not, unpalatable and indigestible.

The novel in all its history has been subject to the winds of commerce, to the customs of society, to the whims of the censor, and to the wild adventures of the mind. It changes like the seasons of the year, like the vagaries of the weather, like the configurations of the clouds in the sky. It can create an illusion or destroy a faith. The only predictable certainty about a novel, no matter what its content or form or purpose, is its ability to arouse the emotions and inject terrifying or comforting ideas into the mind.

From this art of fiction come laughter and tears, despair and inspiration, education and entertainment. For this reason, regardless of a moralizing or demoralizing purpose from year to year and from one generation to the next, its life and vitality is assured as long as emotions rule the heart and ideas invigorate the mind. Only when it is abused and deformed and perverted by ruthless commercialism or political manipulation does the novel lose its penetrating and pervading power of communication.

Even though a precise definition of the novel is elusive because of its changeable nature, certain fundamental characteristics of the novel are readily recognizable.

A fictitious story or tale not previously known can be said to be the basis of a novel, provided that in lengthy exposition it develops a plan to describe and explain the imaginary actions of people in a related sequence of dramatic episodes; and, furthermore, provided that the artistry of the author succeeds in casting a memorable spell upon the heart and mind of the reader. In one novel it may be an incantation of aspiration and inspiration, and in another novel it might be a trance of futility and degradation. Otherwise, the novel is bound to be merely a pallid imitation of life without the spirit of the living.

A novel is many things, because it is its nature to seek and to encompass physical and spiritual life here, there, and everywhere, and its obligation is to see all and to disdain no person or thing. It is a moral tale to inspire those who seek goodness. It is a transcribed dream of vice and immortality to glorify evil. It is a book of mystery, mayhem, and murder; it is war, violence, and death. It is true love and wanton rape. It is people acting out their lives in costumes—cowboys, cockneys, and cocottes; it is people enmeshed in ideas, suppositions, and superstitions. It is life outside the law—horrifying crime performed by the abnormal to shock the normal; vicarious lawlessness to appease a slumbering savagery in the sedate. A novel is the life story of the dedicated clergyman, the licentious landlady, the zealous teacher, and, of course, the wayward waitress and the respectable nymphomaniac.

The reasons for reading these tales are as varied and numerous as the items in a variety store. Reading for pleasure, as it is misguidedly and erroneously called, is always inconclusive and unsatisfying and never an end in itself. The aftereffects of such reading would be no more pleasurable than the gluttonous eating of candy to the point of sickness or drinking whisky to the point of nausea.

Satisfaction, education, enjoyment, entertainment are some of the rewards of reading, but obtainable only when the reader is sufficiently integrated and at ease with the author's fictional persons and imaginary circumstances. This can take place when something is known to the reader by personal experience, or by implication, either pleasantly or unpleasantly, and he is impelled by his gregarious nature to act out his own part just as though he himself were actually on the scene.

As a result, provided the reader has become one of the persons involved in the story and can feel his own reaction to what is happening, everything becomes real and lifelike and earnest. He forms likes and dislikes for certain characters in the novel, he has feelings of love and hate, he approves or disapproves of the thought and behavior on the pages, and he associates himself wholeheartedly with the story. In the end, with emotions aroused or spent, he is reluctant to close the book and suffer the pangs of withdrawal. Not all novels can be so successful, but such an effect is possible if the novel was written by a masterful author.

III

If it is easy to understand why novels are read, it still is not easy to understand why a person chooses the writing of fiction for a trade or profesison. Writing is not an instinctive process or activity like the hoarding of string, or the begetting of children, or even like drawing a caricature of the teacher in a school textbook.

The writing of fiction requires more than the ability to install a new typewriter ribbon when the old ribbon becomes dim. It requires patience beyond ordinary human endurance. It requires the determination of a fanatical zealot. It demands specialized training far beyond the curriculum offered by the most advanced and complete educational institutions. And all the time fiction writing is not even a basic need of society, such as food, clothing, and housing.

Authorship demands, and gets, perfection of the word, the sentence, the paragraph, the whole book. It calls for, and gets, minute illustration of thoughts and behavior without the help of drawings, charts, diagrams, and graphs. It has to have constant and unfailing motivation to justify the most casual incident. And, after all this, the whole thing is completely worthless if it does not succeed in converting ink and paper into something more realistic or romantic than the eye can see and likewise creating persons more alive than the living.

It is true that for some fortunate authors there is relative fame to be had, but, even when achieved, it provides no guarantee that it will not be fleeting and passing and after a time cease to be capable of providing a productive incentive. As any author knows by experience, there is always the next novel to be conceived and written, and a previous one, no matter how successful, is not going to be of any help at all when it comes to writing and perfecting the new one.

The desire for a reward of money, or even the need to make a living, might be a reasonable incentive to become a novelist, but, even so, an author and his money are quickly parted. For one thing, an old friend will appear and tell a masterful, heart-rending, sad tale that wins him a substantial gift of the author's money. For another thing, as it is bound to happen, somebody more astute in the ways of finance and commerce will come along and unload a worthless investment on the poor fellow. Then, too, even if the inexperienced author should be lucky enough to avoid the pitfall of the stock market or a real estate syndicate, he still has to reckon with income tax liens and the deficit financing of alimony payments.

There must be some good reason why an otherwise normal and reasonably rational person is impelled to take upon himself the practice of the profession of writing instead of taking up the traditionally lucrative practice of law or medicine or politics. Even though he may be motivated by his heart's desire, such a person, especially one with supposedly superior talent, would certainly be aware of the hardships lurking around the corner. Libraries are stacked with volumes of authentic history written by the disillusioned which give positive warning of the unhappy endings that are suitable for fiction, but which are too harsh an injustice to inflict upon a human being.

However, no amount of discouragement or adverse advice is going to be persuasive enough when there is fire in the heart and a fever in the mind. This may sound like a trifling figure of speech and might not always be accepted as convincive reasoning, and admittedly it is far from being a realistic reason, yet it is all that is needed to make the urge for writing forever consuming and unquenchable. Perhaps, after all, neither fame nor fortune is the aim and driving force of authorship.

There is only one more likely explanation left. A writer is someone who likes his work, who is happy in the performance of it, and who takes pride in its accomplishment. Such a person rarely fails to make a success in any craft or profession.

IV

Contemporary standards of reading and writing are what are to be expected in this day and age of the extremes of the esthetic and the commercial. As one draws farther away from the other as if in abhorrance of each other's ideals, the esthetic, which might be described in a generality as being a thin volume of esoteric poetry, becomes more and more estranged and alienated from the commercial—which is best described as being at the moment a crass catalog of sexual aberrations. When the paths of the two do cross, it is not surprising, as one tries to outdo the other, that the reader is bombarded by a double-barrelled blast of abnormality and perversion and then threatened with the cross-fire of the abstruse and unintelligible.

In the present stage of civilization, in this era of materialism, the non-profit esthete has to be subsidized in order to survive. It costs money to promote and collect a subsidy, which in turn requires a subsidized payroll for administrators, and even that has to be furnished by a subsidized benefactor. By the time this rifling of pockets is finished, there is next to nothing left for the non-profit esthete. However, the commercial pays its own way and is organized to return a generous profit to the publisher and sometimes, to the author. Commercial publishing is constantly alert to profit possibilities. So alert it is, that publishers are eager to spend money to seek ways to improve methods of research so as to discover and provide increasing margins of profit. It was not so long ago that strictly scientific research established the fact that the most consistently popular and profitable books published year after year were those which extolled the virtues of Abraham Lincoln, family doctors, and faithful dogs.

This scientific break-through was the first important discovery, since the invention of movable type, to benefit the book publishing business. As soon as this discovery was made known, it was inevitable that all alert publishers began commissioning authors to drop everything else and hurry up and write books about the psychological musing of Lincoln's doctor's dog. Later, of course, it became fashionable to debunk the dog and he was exposed as having secretly been a chicken-eater all that time instead of being an expert rat-catcher.

This type of literary research has never since ceased in its efforts to find ways and means to insure larger and larger sales of books. Expansion-of-the-market was its slogan, every man-in-the-street was a sales prospect, and a foot-long list of super best-sellers its goal. With the continued advancement of the science of research in this field, combined with the proven commercial know-how of certain recent novels, it can be anticipated that before long there will be a rash of books written about Lincoln's doctor's girl-friend's poodle. The thinking in the high places of publishing is that the elite of the nation—that is, the two-poodle mistresses—will insure a booming sale of such books with their enthusiastic word-of-mouth advertising.

The first such novel about the doggish traits and psychoses of the kept-woman's poodle may be interesting enough, but the second, third, and thousandth that follow are likely to be merely boring and repetitious. However, by that time, as history is constantly recording, the seemingly dull and boring can suddenly become sensational and daring overnight.

There is well-established precedent for this. It will take place because the censors, both amateur and professional, alarmed by the popularity of a book about a dog, will begin a frantic search for obscure obscenity and overtones of immorality on the printed pages. This is when it becomes widely rumored that the novel is suspect and under investigation, and the stampede to the bookstores is on.

What happens next is that thousands of readers will soon be chagrined to find themselves, after avid and feverish scanning, with just another book about a dog on their hands. Most people already know all they ever care to know about the impulsive motives and stubborn habits of dogs. What they would probably prefer to read is a scandalous novel about a fellow citizen who has the reputation for being a whiz at finding something to suppress before anybody else thought of it.

Censorship is an antisocial force impeding the progress of civilization. After generations of struggling upward, what by now would otherwise be considered a matter of personal taste and public custom becomes instead a denial of freedom of choice to the many for the prejudice of the few. Morals of people are nurtured by the experiences of life and the lessons learned by living become the accepted standards and customs. Other than wife-swappers and husband-traders, almost every person conforms to some extent to tradition and mores, thereby proving that he takes pride in the ideals of society. The imposition of censorship by decree and force is a denial of an individual's right to be master of his fate.

It is not a tenet of civilization to dictate to all an unvarying uniform style of dress and thought and behavior. Good taste in dress and behavior has a habit of prevailing in the end, and vulgarity in thought and act has a long tradition of failing to succeed in popularity.

Reading is education, and from childhood to manhood, year by year and step by step, a person is influenced and guided by parent, teacher, and his own acquired knowledge in the pursuit of learning. After such a time he is capable of knowing and selecting the good from the bad, and he is entitled to the freedom, as an educated person, to choose what he wishes to read. The banning and prohibition of books by the prejudice of censorship becomes a denial of social and educational rights of liberty and freedom.

The intentions of censorship may be sincere and high-minded, but the application of it as a social policy is outmoded. People themselves are the qualified judges of what is right by tradition and what is wrong by custom. Obscenity and vulgarity are matters of bad taste and are not welcomed where decorum and propriety exist. Pornography is something else. It is a condition of psychic malady that can be alleviated by prescribed doses of erotic laxative. The pornographic has the curative properties of a prescribed drug, when taken as directed, and serves a moral purpose when it purges the mind of latent aberrations. The purification of the mind serves this moral purpose by eliminating potential harmful reactions. It is for this same reason that static electricity is grounded and discharged at periodic intervals to prevent dangerous explosions.

All through history erotic relics have been left to become landmarks in the trek of civilization. These landmarks are valuable specimens and scientific evidence of the progress of civilization that are equally as important to the anthropologist and archaeologist as the artifacts found in the trash piles of our primitive ancestors. For this reason alone, it should be clear that civilization itself acts to reject and eliminate social customs as well as to create and perpetuate them.

V

The novel is perhaps the most recently evolved form of writing, and, with poetry, is considered to be a creative art. History and biography preceded the novel and long ago established the dignity of writing. Now a form of autobiography, which is usually an outlandish combination of fact and fantasy, has been invented to provide a neurotic peep show to pacify the psychotic prone.

A close inspection of this self-exposure novelty reveals that the neo-autobiography is actually fiction in disguise while pretending to be personally sincere and factually authentic. The biographer would be quickly called to account if he were found guilty of falsifying the facts of another person's life. But the new brand of autobiographer is under no restraint whatsoever. The book he is writing is supposedly the true story of his own life and, if it is a dull and unexciting existence, he takes the licence to enliven it by invention and imagination and fanciful revelations.

There are as many examples of meandering imagination and fantasy as there are the number of neo-autobiographical books published.

One such example to be suspicious of is the autobiography of a self-styled literary figure who gleefully describes himself as being the illegitimate son of a career-woman mother and an obscure phlegmatic bus driver who were marooned one night in a snow-drift between Denver and Omaha. He would have readers believe that when he was a mere child he was placed in a military school and beaten with sabers every night until he cried himself to sleep. In another chapter it is revealed in bitter language that his career-woman mother was violently angry and annoyed when he, in the throes of acute homesickness at the age of fifteen, visited her unexpectedly one week end while she was entertaining a lover who was introduced as being a railroad conductor on the Chicago-Buffalo run. As the consequence of this, he reveals that he barely survived arsenic poisoning after eating several slices of chocolate cake she baked for him.

Further, in what is described as a psychological act of filial love motivated by psychopathic retaliation, the autobiography gives a full and detailed account of his becoming an airline pilot on the Boston-Dallas flight segment and having his first love affair with a woman who was the exact age of his mother. As to be expected, he promptly deserted her at the first sign of pregnancy. Obviously, all this is intended to be an esoteric explanation of a cycle in life that comes to all men, and, of course, with cosmic implications.

The reader comes next to the chapter in the autobiography which gives a tear-stained description of his pitifully unsuccessful career trying to sell under-the-counter stocks and bonds to widows, imported bat manure to suburban housewives, and foreign stag films for home movies.

The final portion of this weeping-heart autobiography is, naturally, devoted to a happy ending. This reveals the true story of his fortunate marriage to the second richest girl in the world and of his happiness in finding true love at last. There is something plausible about this, particularly when he says that she gave him ten thousand dollars to print ten thousand copies of his autobiography for free distribution to ten thousand close and intimate friends who had become attached to his personality.

The very last chapter of this autobiography describes the author's vision of the future. Now that he has firmly established himself in the exciting world of literature, as he expresses it, and has been able to wipe from memory all filial recollection of his career-woman mother, he has taken a solemn vow to devote the remainder of his life to creating novels of social significance and composing volumes of lyrical poetry in praise of the common man.

IX. WHAT READERS

OUGHT TO KNOW ABOUT WRITERS

Unlike most actors and politicians, whose faces and grimaces are familiar sights on television screens and outdoor billboards, authors may sometimes become known to the general public by name and reputation, but it is not often that they would be recognized by facial features or forensic gestures.

As it could happen when a locally-known author is called upon to give his name and state his occupation to a police officer or census taker in his home town, the official might display a sort of delayed reaction, or double-take, accompanied by a suspicious frown.

After moments of thoughtful silence and then another quick look by the police officer or census taker, the inevitable question would be:

"Are you really THE Tommy Turnipseed?"

It makes no difference at all after that whether the author is actually the Turnipseed or just any Turnipseed.

There is no time for him to think of a clever quip or epigram and, besides, the officer has already made up his mind that you are either an imposter or one of those no-account Turnipseeds who are always scrounging around after dark for firewood and hen eggs. Under such circumstances, and pressed for an immediate answer, the author has to say the first thing that comes to mind.

"Well, if there's anybody else with the same name, he is no kin to me."

When the police officer or census taker goes home that night, he will have a good laugh with his wife.

"A funny thing happened today. I was asking a fellow the usual questions, and do you know what he did?"

"What did he do?"

"He tried to claim he was Tommy Turnipseed."

"You mean THE Tommy Turnipseed?"

"Exactly. But he didn't fool me for one second."

"Why not?"

"Because he couldn't think of anything to say that I couldn't have said quicker and funnier. Besides, he didn't even look like a writer."

"What did he look like?"

"Just like me or anybody else you come across."

The most difficult thing for a writer to accomplish in life is to be able to look like one. Even the traditional theory that it takes one to know one is impractical and unreliable. A physician is easily identified with his profession by his stylish high-button white jacket, a lawyer is always known by the four inches of protruding shirt cuffs, and a dentist is immediately recognized in any crowd by his snaggle-tooth smile.

But an author is never quite sure how to display the cachet of his profession and set himself apart in such a manner that he would not be mistaken for an ordinary person who reads books.

Various experiments have been made in the past by the most imaginative authors to devise an insignia that would be universally recognizable at first sight as the badge of authorship. Some writers have undertaken to wear beards, some resort to smoking pipes, and others become addicted to blondes. However, in actual practice, none of these appurtenances or appendages have succeeded in becoming an authentic signet. The trouble was that the writer with a beard was usually mistaken for a skidrow bum, the pipe smoker was often mistaken for a hospital intern, and the one with the blonde was always mistaken for a ready-to-wear salesman at a dress goods convention at Miami Beach.

In order to clarify the confusion, it would seem that the best way for a writer to give the appearance of being one is to put smudges of typewriter ribbon under his fingernails, clip a solid-gold autograph pen to his coat lapel, and always wear a pencil-stripe suit. And another thing: casually flip the pages of a leather-bound book when appearing in public.

When an author is so recognized, for instance in his natural habitat, the cocktail party, the ordinary reader should be sure to follow certain rules of approach and conduct. For one thing, you should always introduce yourself with equal amounts of humility, obeisance, and self-depreciation. Next, you should put the author in good humor by telling him that you have heard of him all your life, but that you never expected to have the good fortune to meet him in person and actually shake his hand. An example of this procedure would be as follows:

"I'm just a common, ordinary, average, everyday reader, and I couldn't write the first line of a story if my life depended on it. But I knew you were somebody of literary importance when I saw smudges of typewriter ribbon under your fingernails, that solid-gold autograph pen clipped to your coat lapel, and that handsome leather-bound book in your hand. And of course I knew that an author like you would be wearing a pencil-stripe suit."

The author will undoubtedly look upon you with a congenial smile and lift his glass in a salute of fellowship. You are certain that you are going to have a memorable coversation when the author leans forward and asks:

"What have you read lately?"

"I read your last novel."

"It was not my last novel! That happens to be my most recent novel!"

"Well, I'm awfully sorry. I didn't mean what I said to sound like that. I'm just an ordinary reader, you know, and I'm not very good at using the right words the way you do. But please believe me. I liked your recent novel very much. It was really great. And that was a wonderful title you picked out for it. *Rosie Redhead.* I always did say that you never fail to come up with catchy titles for your novels. It takes real genius to do that every time."

"I did not write that book!"

"You didn't? But I thought your name was Turnipseed."

"My name is Turnipseed—Tommy Turnipseed. That so-called novel you mentioned was written by some impostor who deceives the public by turning out books under the unscrupulous pseudonym of Johnny Turnipseed."

"Well, I guess there are a lot of Turnipseeds in the world, and it's hard for an ordinary reader like me to know one from the other."

"Look here! Are you inferring that I have a peculiar name?"

"No! I didn't mean it to sound like that. Honest, I didn't. After all, I'm just an ordinary reader—"

"Good-by!"

"Good-by, Mr. Turnipseed."

"Tommy Turnipseed! THE Tommy Turnipseed!"

II

It would not be politic to make an open book of the secret lives of authors. It would be most unbecoming to invade their private domain and reveal to all the nature of their conduct behind the closed doors of their homes. The reason for this reticence is that it has long been considered to be a traditional privilege for them to have the exclusive use of such intimate personal revelations for publication in their autobiographies. However, it would be in the public interest to make known as far as possible something about the nature of the curious pastimes or hobbies in which they are suspected of indulging.

It may come as a surprise to the ordinary reader, since it is not generally known to outsiders, but the fact is that authors seek escape and surcease from the confining drudgery of their work and find gratification in the most unusual hobbies. This has been a well-kept secret in the profession for many years.

Being by nature disinclined to conform to the common customs, which is to say being eccentric, writers are constantly striving to devise pastimes which they consider to be appropriate for their status and unlikely to be indulged in by ordinary readers. This is why authors are rarely, if ever, seen on golf courses, at civic club luncheons, in the neighborhood sporting house. As a consequence of this, there is the wide-spread belief, which by now is almost legendary, that writers actually think they are too superior to associate socially wth any person who is merely an ordinary reader. The excuse they usually make for this attitude is that they are afraid to take the risk of becoming hopelessly addicted to commonplace pastimes.

It should not be unreasonable to let writers have the same privileges that eccentric citizens in other crafts and professions are granted without question. That is to say, writers should be permitted, just like any other eccentric, to indulge in their hobbies and pastimes within the privacy of their own homes and beyond the prying eyes of gossiping readers.

It is probably assumed by most readers that the secret hobbies and pastimes of writers are stamp collecting, wood carving, leather tooling, butterfly mounting, pool shooting, and cat breeding. This is far from being the case. Authors consider themselves too individualistic and imaginative to spend their free time taking part in the commonplace pastimes that have come to be associated with ordinary readers.

It is not likely that any author will ever reveal the precise nature of his favorite, or clandestine, hobby for all the world to know. For one thing, he fears that if his particular hobby were made known to the ordinary readers in the world that it would become so popular that he would lose the image of his personality when publically identified with it. For another thing, he is afraid that if his secret pastime becomes known to cynical literary critics, they will take delight in writing satiric comments about the unusual way he spends his time in private. A few authors, it is true, have been persuaded by their publishers to divulge such secrets in their autobiographies, but they turned out to be nothing more than confessions that they were addicted to crocheting and knitting.

However, since no names will be revealed and no identity intimated, there is nothing improper in divulging, in a strictly professional manner, a few typical secret hobbies or pastimes of authors. In doing so, many erroneous ideas, suppositions, and suspicions can be dislodged from the minds of readers.

What goes on behind the author's locked doors and drawn curtains may seem childlike and undignified, if not downright ridiculous, but it must be remembered that the sole purpose of a hobby is to provide relaxation and gratification with as little mental stress and strain as possible.

In other words, the hobby or pastime should always be simple and never complex. This rules out anything like trying to put square pegs into round holes or learning to finger paint on window panes. Most important of all, however, the hobby should be such that it can be quickly and easily moved or dismounted, and at the same time be small and collapsible so it can be concealed on a moment's notice in a desk drawer or under the couch when an unexpected visitor arrives.

Now it can be readily assumed that these exacting conditions immediately eliminate such obvious pastimes as cabinet making, rug weaving, cake baking, taxidermy, and playing with electric trains. By ruling out such hobbies as these from guess and conjecture, the field has been considerably narrowed. Admittedly, there is little else left for an author to do in secret; perhaps this is why most of them spend all their time writing.

III

It is sometimes wondered why there are such large numbers of authors who devote themselves exclusively to writing what is known in the trade as juvenile fiction or junior books. In particular, it is often wondered why a well-known author of sophisticed novels of sex and mayhem will startle the literary world by publishing a simple-minded story for pre-school children who have not yet learned to read, but whose mothers are thrilled by the colorful illustrations that smear with the touch of a finger. As it happens, there is good and sufficient reason for a novelist to stop in the middle of a serious work and turn out some story-books for mommie and the little ones.

For instance, there is the case of the novelist who was told by his publisher in a grave heart-to-heart session that the sales of his books had become disastrously small and that something drastic had to be done about it at once.

In a publisher's diplomatic way, it was suggested that the author's recent adult novels had offended the sensibilities of lady librarians and booksellers throughout the nation. Using a careful choice of words and speaking ingratiatingly, this is how he explained the somber situation to the novelist:

"A recent survey made by the publishing industry shows that eight out of ten librarians and booksellers from coast to coast are elderly, prudish, straight-laced spinsters of the old-school who are easily offended and shocked by the excessive frankness and realism of modern fiction. Of course, you understand that I am completely objective and I would never be influenced personally by such an old-fashioned attitude. However, since these nice old ladies—any one of whom might have been your mother or mine—well, since they do have the authority to reject books for their school and public libraries and can refuse to stock them in the bookshops, it would be wise, and good business for both of us, if you kept this in mind when you write your next novel."

As is to be expected, the novelist was deeply affronted by the obvious commercial motives of the publisher. Bristling in a huff, this is what he said in reply:

"Look here, Max! I'll have you know that I resent such a suggestion and I absolutely refuse to prostitute my art by writing drivel for a flock of old biddies. But wait a minute, Max! I know how to get even with them. You just wait and see."

Fired by enthusiasm and boiling with resentment, the author goes home and dashes off a story-book for pre-school children and their mommies. Naturally, the exciting story is about a fussy old hen who has a brood of chicks.

As the story opens, it is established that the old biddy is always tormenting and pecking at the young pullets and cockerels. Then one day there is an uprising in the chicken house and open rebellion by the young poults against the old hen and her henpecking domination and harassment. The outcome is that every last one of the fledgling broilers fly the coop. The lonely old biddy is downhearted and contrite, but she knows it is too late to make amends, and her sorrow is so devastating that she begins to molt. She makes a sorry-looking sight, shedding her feathers and clucking pathetically, as she scratches diffidently in the barnyard.

Sympathy for the poor old biddy has now been firmly established in the tender minds and hearts of the pre-school brats and their mommies. And so now it is precisely at this psychological moment that an unexpected and startling complication arises which threatens the very existence of the old biddy.

The farmer comes along at this particular stage of the story with his shiny hatchet, muttering to himself that he has a craving for chicken stew with dumplings. It is obvious now that he is going to cull the droopy old hen. But, just in time, the farmer's wife happens to be passing the barnyard and she sees the molted old biddy's wrinkly neck on the chopping block.

Well! The farmer's wife tells the farmer that it would take more time than she can spare from her chores to stew a tough old hen and, besides, she tells him, a plump poulard or capon would make a much tastier chicken stew with dumplings. The farmer has learned by years of experience that, if he hopes to have dumplings with his chicken stew, he had better pay attention to his wife when she speaks to him.

So, under the circumstances, there is only one wise course for him to take. He puts the clucking old moulted hen into a crate and ships her off to the old biddie's home where she lives happily ever after.

Of course, the story-book is read by all the lady librarians and booksellers from one end of the country to the other, and they become so enthralled over the heart-rending symbolism of the fable that they order thousands of copies from the publisher.

Naturally, this makes the story-book an immediate runaway best-seller and it earns so much money for the author that never again does he have to waste his time and talent writing sophisticated novels of sex and mayhem for grown-ups. And this is why there are so many authors these days writing story-books for pre-school brats and their mommies.

X. FODDER AND

FONDUE IN FICTION

It is always so much in fashion nowadays either to depreciate to the depths of irrationality or to praise to the heights of absurdity that the normal elements and the great common ground of fiction are in danger of being ignored and dismissed as being unworthy of notice. This vogue for the worship of the literary extreme, like the political precepts of the ultra-conservative and the ultra-radical, has become the impassioned doctrine of the contemporary American novel and short story.

It could be that a peculiar literary diet of fodder and fondue is responsible for the present-day glorification of excessive sensationalism and inordinate asceticism. This results in the mass production of sexy mayhem for the hopelessly hooked addict of the sensual and narcissistic graphics for the emotionally inhibited.

Sophisticated fashions and scholarly vogues being what they are, it is usually only the maverick writer or a defiant author who has the courage and spirit to go against the trend of the moment and prove by challenge that the art of fiction is the rightful heritage of all and is not to be confined to esoteric indulgence by the few.

The time has passed in this world when only the royalists and landed gentry had the leisure to be writers and readers. The time has passed into history, and with even more quickened tempo since the industrial revolution in the western world, when only the rich could afford the luxury of being writers and readers. In those times, ambition and talent were held to be the exclusive birthright of the socially and economically priviledged.

The time now appears to be one in which the magacephalic branch of the human race is attempting to reserve the reading and writing of fiction for an exclusive privilege of its members in a psychotic world of sophisticated self-gratification. Or, in more moderate language, it can be described as a society for the promotion and establishment of a literary daisy chain.

In contemporary America, theoretically, every literate person has the opportunity to become a writer or the privilege of being a reader. Literally, this theory has come to be taken for granted as an indisputable and inalienable right. Consequently, with such democratic freedom in action, the grave danger here is the likelihood that writers will outnumber readers.

Reduced to prosaic terms of economics, what this indicates is that the supply of writers will soon, if not already, far exceed the demand. This imbalance of supply and demand will have to be adjusted by some means, perhaps simply by drawing straws, if the market is ever going to be stabilized. Otherwise, the time will surely come when everybody is busy writing his novel and there will not be a single reader left to buy a book.

However, what is to be considered at this time is more important than the matter of surplus authors. After all,

with proper guidance and a few stringent laws, the interest of unemployed writers can be diverted to reading.
The principal concern here has to do with the two extremes of unjustifiable depreciation and unwarranted
praise and the resulting effects upon writer and reader
alike.

In the course of recent years, readers have frequently
been misled by fulsome praise of mediocre novels and by
defamatory criticism of superior fiction. This imbalance,
likewise, is in need of adjustment.

A principal reason for these extreme and intemperate
pronouncements may be due to the fact that the former
anonymous and professionally qualified book reviewer
has been forced into unemployment by the flamboyant,
first-person-singular, by-line critic. The latter's interest in
books is solely for the purpose of finding pellets to be used
in slingshot-worded marksmanship aimed to enhance his
own literary image.

As to be expected, this questionable change in literary
emphasis has led, first, to parochial propaganda to disparage the traditions of the past and, finally, to unqualified
praise of sensational and merely topical fiction in book
and magazine. As a result of this, the reader is soon sur-
feited by the sensational and transitory, just as he has
been in times past by art-for-art's sake and other fashionable rages, and he is hard put to it to find the emotionally sincere and close-to-home fiction which he seeks
and to which he is entitled.

Engaged in an occupation similar to that of the flamboyant journalist, and equally in fault, there is to be
found the scholarly essayist who becomes academically
absorbed and heavy-footed in the mire of his own brilliant
semantics. His verbiage is usually shined and polished to
a sparkling luster, and it is frequently a model for the
cloistered study of symbolism and narcissism and other
literary by-products of the craft of fiction. As it is, though,

neither on gleaming surface nor in plumbable depth, is he able to offer helpful insight or a guiding hand to reader or writer. In other words, the scholarly essayist succeeds in saying nothing in a classical manner.

On average, like his journalistic counterpart, the scholarly essayist carefully avoids the great common ground of life. He can usually be found retreating in a flurry of obscure and involved language to a nether world of depreciation or to the never-never land of extravagant praise. As if by a whim of nature, he appears to have an abiding fear of using the common language of fellow men.

As a result of these peculiarities of literary criticism, a wide gap of common ground separates the fictionized case history of a criminal pervert and the solar plexus meditation of the psychotic intellectual, to name only two of the extreme examples, from the four-letter pornography of the pseudo-sophisticate and the finger-painted graphics of the neo-primitive. This expansive chasm has left a whole area of life and letters untended and abandoned.

It is now too late to reclaim the past. The damage has been done. A miraculous totality of recall would not be an effective substitute. Even faithful and industrious historical research would only result in a pallid imitation of that era. Fiction is only partly a product of recollection, anyway, and it is capable of being expressive and provocative, arousing and inspiring, only when infused with imagination and expertly blended with living emotions and creative talent.

Contemporaneous subjects and recognizable scenes and keen observation of living persons are the basic materials of enduring and meaningful fiction. Masters of storytelling always write of the times in which they live and faithfully record the economic, social, and political pressures and effects of such an era upon the lives and character of the persons they create.

Perception of all things by the author is of the first

order. When this is achieved, the refining of impressions, the signifying of motivations, and the presentation of implications will constitute the soul of the writer's art. This, when fulfilled, is meaningful storytelling at its best. As a result, the emotions and intellect of the reader will respond to such consummate art with aversion and abomination or, as the case may be, he will react with sympathy and compassion. Such is the event of artistic creation and communication.

Narration, description, and dialogue are the shiny gadgets and optional accessories of the vehicle. Wheels and motive power and a guiding hand are the fundamental essentials for conveyance.

II

There was a time in America not so long ago, and that era is still a memorable one to a great many persons, when the novel was considered to be a pernicious influence. It was widely denounced as a thing of evil and characterized as an instrument of the devil. Religious conviction banned it and the righteous shunned it. And even more than being a frivolous pastime, reading fiction was considered in some places to be an unpardonable sin. In such an atmosphere, there was no such thing as a good novel; literary merit was not even an acceptable excuse for reading it.

Yet, somehow, it perhaps being the way of the world, fiction continued to be written and published, more and more year by year, and the reading of novels and short stories ceased to be confined to the atheist and agnostic and back-slider. This was the time when even the most devout churchgoer began reading novels and magazine short stories behind locked doors and hiding them from the sight of prying eyes by storing them under the mattress. Swapping of nickel-dreadfuls and dime-novels in the alley and behind the post office came to be a Saturday night custom so as to provide fresh reading matter for Sunday afternoon.

In the course of time, fictional books and magazines gradually came out of hiding and the religious or moral ban was progressively relaxed or rescinded. Soon it became fashionable to build bookshelves and to display magazines on reading table. By then it had become a sign of culture and social distinction to read and own and talk about current fiction. Volumes were bound in cloth and leather and the price started upward. Neighborhood literary clubs were organized and ladies' reading societies began to flourish.

Then something happened along the way. The freedom to read novels without guilt had become a social and cultural obsession in American life. Every parent who could afford the expense wanted his son and daughter to attend college and be instructed in a fashionable selection of fiction and to acquire an appreciation of literature.

The trouble about this was that the college and university of the time were not prepared to offer courses of instruction in the American novel and short story. The textbooks on the subject were inadequate, and in most instances the professor was at a loss in knowing how to proceed in the teaching of the appreciation of native American fiction.

Until that time, poetry and essays had been the recognized and accepted contribution to American literature, and the teacher had scarcely more knowledge and understanding of native fiction than the student. Consequently, the only fiction in which the teacher could provide instruction was that which had been written by British authors, and such was the substitution. It was a sad state of affairs.

Neither professors nor colleges were wholly at fault

for being unprepared for this sudden concerted effort by
students to obtain literary culture. It was an abrupt and
surprising turnabout for American fiction to become acceptable and respectable. It had been in disrepute for a
long time and had the firmly established reputation for
being behind-locked-doors and under-the-mattress scatol-
ogy. And having for so long a time been held in low
esteem, it provided another good reason for substituting
and hastily accrediting the British novel for study in place
of the American novel. Besides, all fiction from that
mother country was considered to be in good taste and
endowed with the highest standards of literary quality.
It was accepted without question that the English or
Scottish novel had no taint of behind-locked-doors im-
propriety and under-the-mattress immorality.

Over the years, and solely by reason of this quirk of
circumstance, the works of British authors came to be
standard fare for proper reading and the model of literary
perfection. As a result, American authors went unread
and unappreciated in colleges and universities and so
came to be branded as unworthy of study and recognition.

And that was not all. Things eventually went so far
that English and Scottish authors, like Swiss yodelers and
bell-ringers, became a popular attraction on American
tours. Their personal appearances on lecture platforms
became cultural events from one side of the nation to
the other. They received grand receptions by society and
universities, and, incidently, the momentous sales of their
books enabled them to carry heavy moneybags all the
way back to Britain. And to this day, British authors have
a kindly feeling toward Americans and a deep appreciation for their generosity.

In the nineteen-thirties there was an historic economic
depression in the United States. During most of that
decade, no part of the nation was spared from the blight.
The flow of money trickled to an end. Lecture tours of

British authors were cancelled. American editions of British novels went unbought. There was social and economic unrest in the land. It was no time to think of the cultural values of literature when there was hunger in the stomach. People were concerned with their immediate physical needs. Food, clothing, and shelter dominated thought and action; imported culture could wait.

And then gradually, one by one in the beginning, American novels depicting that era of desperation and despair and despondency began to appear. After that, with increasing momentum, American novelists and short story writers, who had been scorned and ignored and rejected during those years of the imported cultural binge, were read and understood and appreciated.

People wanted to read about themselves, about their relatives, about their fellow citizens in this time of travail and hardship. This was the one way they could see their lives in true perspective. And readers were not disappointed in what they found was being written by this new generation of native writers.

Novelists were writing in a language that everybody could understand—the American language—and they were able to reveal and interpret the true character of the American people for the first time. These books were hard and tough and relentless in wording and content; some were clumsy and awkward and misshapen; but all of them were revealing and unrestrained.

Within a few short years, the American novel had come to life. The British novel was no longer a matrix and model. Now there were native novels for native readers. And the American writer had come into his own.

Such was the beginning, and the new age was to continue for a long time afterward. With the coming of realism, for three decades a true appreciation of the American novelist gripped the country. As a result of this, the first enduring native tradition in fiction had been established. More than that, and deservedly, appreciation of this new writing began spreading over the world. Its startling vitality had no limits.

All this is in the past now, and the complete chapter has been written into history.

The present time is that of several decades since the birth and first resounding strides of modern American fiction. And apparently something has gone wrong. All is not as it was in time past.

Perhaps the first major crop of fiction of the country has come to maturity and is no longer thriving and prolific. Nevertheless, the same fertile soil remains. And now and then there are signs and indications of a springtime stirring in the fallow ground and a likelihood of another abundant harvest to come.

III

Economic turmoil, political upheavals, and the inevitable tragedies of war have been powerful incentives in the past that incited and inspired the writing of major fiction. Now in contemporary America there is a new challenge to all young writers that holds the promise of even greater fulfillment in the future. This is a challenge to dramatize and interpret and give meaningful direction to the unresolved economic and racial inequalities. The power of writing is capable of furnishing the necessary leadership.

First of all, assuming that preparation for any challenge is desirable, the young writer should reject the invitation to become a member of the incestuous household of a literary claque. The reason for this is clear. It is a subversive act and a perversion of criticism to entice an author into writing by prescribed rules. The true function of criticism is to make an impartial and impersonal evaluation of a work after it has been written and published.

Next, the young writer should acquire the strength of character to enable him to assume the responsibility of being and acting as an individual. Team work is desirable and frequently necessary for the success of a research project in science or letters, but the creation of a novel is more apt to take place in the lonely attic of the mind.

And, thirdly, the young writer should beware of imitating the work of another writer, no matter how admirable it may be, for this will surely lead to the dead-end of creative ability and eventually to unpardonable plagiary.

Only in this way will a young writer be able to escape from the plague of prescribed thought—or follow the leader—and remain free to explore the whole domain of life.

For some time now there has been a scornful and disdainful attitude in some quarters toward regional writing and, in particular, a contemptuous criticism directed at the regional author himself. In such quarters of criticism, a perceptive regional novel by an outsider will often be dismissed and belittled with the charge that it is an amateurish nonentity by an amateurish scribbler who has the misfortune to be concerned with his own hinterland. Knowing the source, it is enough to say that such criticism is an indication of ignorance or is motivated by professional jealousy.

Regional fiction, which can be either provincial or urban in locality, or a combination of both, covers that great common ground which exists between the currently fashionable pastime of meditating on the solar plexus and, at the other extreme, exalting compatible homosexuality.

For one thing, it is erroneous to think of regional fiction as being geographically or psychologically remote from human life and activity. Correctly, it is a descriptive term to identify a concentration of life and activity in any particular part of the country. For instance, such a region with attendant conflicts could be Boston, Philadelphia, the Ozarks, the Oklahoma Panhandle, a Rocky Mountain intervale, or a small town on the Natchez Trace.

Likewise, regional fiction is not confined to chronicles of marital spats on a back-country farm, to quaint family feuds among mountaineers, and to local abberations in a brackish bayou. There is drama, conflict, tragedy, and comedy wherever people live—in the slums of New York, in the high-rise apartments of Chicago, and throughout the stucco jungles of Los Angeles.

Regional fiction has always been the lever-and-wedge of American literature. More than any other kind of writing, it keeps the records for, and makes the interpretation of, the social and racial structure of the nation. It is the vivid history of the folkways of the country; it is the personal diary of the people.

The typical American, if there might be such a person, or a composite American, which there may never be, would in theory be a man of many heritages. He would be a compound of the Scandinavian of the North, the Negro of the South, the Mexican of the West, and the European of the East. But as long as there is a lingering tradition of racial integrity resisting amalgamation, there can be no typical or composite American, and the regions where people live will remain distinctive and fertile with the rich materials of fiction. It should not be surprising if one of these regions inspired the writing of the mythical great American novel.

There is a tendency among those who are unaware of the distinctive quality of regional life to write into history the conjecture that American civilization is standardized and all of a pattern. This is far from being truth and fact. Living habits and customs are constantly changing with the times and the restless movement of families from place to place never ceases, but regional traditions are quickly assimilated and will generate a powerful pull of emotional gravity. Wandering Americans rarely lock in their hearts the sentiment that the home place is always back-home.

Even a uniformity of television programs, a mass circulation of national magazines, and the rapidity of transportation have not succeeded in altering the essential spirit and nature of regional life. Each distinctive region continues to cling tenaciously to its traditions and eventually absorbs invading ideas and converts the gadgets of standardization to its own particular use. It proudly maintains the localized nuances of dialect and vernacular.

And this is not all. The soil and the products of the soil remain. The climate continues to be unyielding harsh or benignly mild. The tall trees grow where they have always grown; scrawny vegetation persists in struggling for survival in its native ground. The muddy Mississippi, the dusty course of the Rio Grande, the sluggish tide of the Columbia, the sky-blue flow of the Kennebec—all these timeless symbols are constant reminders of the enduring nature of regional America and the powerful strength of its emotional gravity on its people.

IV

The world of fiction is composed of the writer, the publisher, the critic, and the reader. Of these, the ultimate depositary is the reader and, wherever freedom of choice exists, it is he who makes the decision to accept or reject what has been written and offered by publication. In a completely regulated state, it is not the privilege of the reader to accept or reject; it is a social and economic necessity as a political citizen to accede to the distate of the state. The state itself is both the prescribing critic and the printing press for what it chooses to publish.

In a completely free state, it is the custom for the publisher to be the custodian of the printing press for the benefit of all. It would be unrealistic to think, however,

that any publisher in America always provides a criterion
of literary judgment. In fact, the publisher is engaged in
a private commercial enterprise with a profit motive. His
success and reputation as a publisher depend upon his
ability to select for publication and offer for sale those
books which readers choose to buy and read.

Whenever the publisher is accused of issuing so-called
trashy or immoral or obscene books, or even pornographic
publications, the odium rightly should be directed at the
readers who create the demand for them. When a free
press prevails, it is not the province of the publisher to
be a censor, nor should it be the province of the state.
Censorship, when desirable, should be the personal obligation and an individual act motivated by the judgment
of a reader. This means that any reader has the privilege
of rejecting any book, but he should not have the right
to ban it and prevent another reader from exercising his
privilege to accept or reject it. The last thing a commercial publisher would do would be to risk going bankrupt
by printing books which nobody wanted to buy and read.

And when a publisher ventures to issue the first work
of a young writer that proves to have unusual merit, he
is entitled to a token of appreciation, which, unfortunately, he rarely receives.

The reader will always be tempted with offerings of
fodder without nourishing grain, fondue without the bite
of nutrition. The winds of commerce will continue to
swirl with chaff and brings showers of confetti. The make-
believe is a perennial enticement.

Editorship and publishing, however, has much more
than this to offer. On every hand can be found the tracts
and propaganda of the social and political extremists—
the radical conservatives, the radical do-nothings, and
the radical revolutionaries. There are continued new offerings by the angry generation and the rebels in beards.
The printing presses are busy with the writings of the es-

capists, realists, romanticists, conformists, non-conformists, neo-conformists, anti-comformists, nudists, Buddhists, and Marxists.

Out of all this conglomeration of ideas and expositions ranging from aberration to zoomorphism, the one thing certain to emerge year after year is an enduring addition to the library of American fiction.

The fodder and fondue will be forgotten; the chaff and confetti will blow away. What remains will be a record and a revelation of the social, moral, political, and economic history of America and an interpretation of the indigenous life and folkways of its regions. Regardless of extremes, regardless of experimental isms and psychological tics, the great common ground of fiction always sees to it that such things are never left undone. This is the heritage, privilege, and glory of the American novel.

XI. THE ART,

CRAFT, AND PERSONALITY OF WRITING

There was a time not so long ago when the ability to think up stories and write novels was proclaimed to be a manisfestation of supernatural imagination. As a result, it came to be an unwritten law that the privilege to be a writer was a magical blessing bestowed upon a chosen few by some kindly and mysterious overlord.

Naturally, the reason for this state of affairs was because none of those privileged authors wanted to share the rewards of authorship with ordinary writers. It was not surprising that they used all the tricks of their trade to perpetuate this item of folklore in order to discourage and disenchant outsiders and keep them out of the business.

And so it was that the franchised authors in those times past jealously guarded their usurped rights and resisted all efforts of the novice and apprentice to enter the sacrosanct realm of their profitable cartel and monopoly.

However, the universally human desire to be a story-teller and express one's self in print remained alive and restless in the minds and hearts of ambitious visionaries even though in those days there was scant hope of liberation and fulfillment. But as sympathetic fate would have it, it was this very policy of those entrenched authors who monopolized the business of writing that eventually resulted in their undoing.

Thwarted and denied by the selfish-minded and prosperous clique of self-appointed authors, the would-be writer sought some other means that would be an outlet for the bright fires of his literary ambitions.

Burning with resentment and eager to retaliate, it was only natural that he would think of begging and borrowing enough money to start a little magazine of his own. And therein he was able to excoriate, belittle, depreciate, disparage, asperse, vilify, malign, and otherwise give vent to a long accumulation of wrath and frustration. All this gave rise to the commonly accepted theory that if a person is unable to succeed as a fiction writer, at least he can become a critic of those who are fiction writers.

And so this was no doubt the origin of literary criticism as it is known today and the advent of the quarrelsome malcontented as men of letters. These were the same critics who got together and decided that a high-class word was to be applied to the short stories and novels of which they approved. The outcome of this was the introduction of the term literature into the language and ever since it has been consistently used whenever critics congregate. Subsequently, however, this high ideal degenerated somewhat and the inevitable result was the inception of the popular pastime now known universally as book reviewing.

II

It was no wonder then when it became known that the door to the literary life had been opened to all that there was an overwhelming migration of young and old to colleges and universities. This resulted in a mighty clamor for courses of instruction in fiction writing or literary criticism—or at least in book reviewing.

Nobody wanted to study to be a reader and learn to be selective and perceptive and to be able to appreciate what he read. True to a vision of the good life, nearly everybody wanted to be either a prominent author or a renowned critic of authors. The few who were foresighted, however, wisely decided that it would be more realistic to become editors or publishers and be assured of a weekly pay check.

Few places of higher learning were prepared to teach a person how to write a readable short story or novel. One reason for this was because even years of scientific experiments had failed to inject successfully into the veins of eager laboratory volunteers the genii of professional authorship. However, parents who had paid good money for room, board, tuition, and bucket-seat sport cars insisted that the faculty hurry up and teach Son Roscoe and Daughter Betty Sue the art and craft of professional writing and to graduate them in a hurry so they would lose no time in becoming rich and famous authors.

Instructors and professors, all mindful of tenure of office and sabbaticals and the pesty alumni, had no choice but to try to do the best they could under the pressure of the circumstances. Scholarly textbooks were hastily put together, inspiring lectures were delivered, and diagrams of stories and novels in the public domain were mimeographed. And that was not all. Lively jokes were told in class by staid and sedate deans in a desperate effort to alleviate the jittery emotional tenseness of students who were awed to know that they were standing on the threshold of professional authorship.

And that still was not all. Teachers of creative writing courses held seminars in their own homes in the evening so everybody could sit on the floor and drink tea and absorb the classic atmosphere of the literary life. The ritual of reading class-assigned short stories and essays took place in a solemn and respectful attitude. Everybody was inspired and thrilled and confident—everybody, that is, except the professor who considerately kept his doubts to himself. He knew that if it were possible to learn how to write meaningful and publishable short stories and novels without prolonged and dedicated apprenticeship, and with some measure of native ability—well, he would have lost no time in doing it himself.

The process of acquiring and perfecting the art and craft of writing is highly unscientific, obviously not scholarly, and certain to be a drudging ordeal of trial-and-error for nobody knows how long. There are many ways of finding one's way in the pursuit of this speculative and unpredictable occupation. Of them all, the privilege merely to expose the mind in the daily forum of learning is likely to be the most rewarding opportunity the student of writing will find anywhere in life. After that, whatever happens is bound to be either a gift of fortune or a reward for servitude.

III

An understanding of the art of writing can sometimes be acquired by reading the works of the literary masters of the past. The craft of writing can often be learned by a long period of instruction and practice.

By combining these two methods, the art and craft of writing are available to all in several ways—by self-education, by instruction, or merely by paying somebody in

Boston or Philadelphia a hundred dollars for a mail-order correspondence course. And to be practical about it, one way is as good as another for technical purposes. After that, only one step more remains, and that is the proof by performance that the writer has something meaningful or entertaining to say and is able to express it better than anybody else.

Even though none of these possibilities has ever been a guarantee that assures absolute success, they at least may suggest second thoughts to those who might have the idea that writing a book is so easy that they could have written a better one themselves if only they had had the leisure to devote to it. Nothing looks so easy and effortless to accomplish as writing a short story or novel after the experience of reading a rousing and memorable one written by somebody else.

As every aspiring writer eventually comes to know, either by keen perception or by heart-rending effort, the conception and creation of durable fiction is the result of the application of some degree of talent. Where superior talent does exist and is ruggedly trained by perseverance, persistence, and dogged patience, and, furthermore, is motivated by authentic emotional and intellectual urges, the personality of the writer is the essential quality that makes his book distinctive and compelling and acceptable as a work of both art and commerce. This quality is, in a way, an electric charge that makes sparks on contact.

Of course, all is not art in this practical world of commercialized fiction. But when it does exist, there are many different kinds of art. There is authentic art. There is synthetic art. There is obviously contrived art. And there is art that failed.

The most prevalent and conspicuous in these categories of art, however, is the imitation of art. The conscious and deliberate imitation of another writer's style and treatment of a subject is always recognizable by the absence of any emotional sympathy or intellectual feeling whatsoever. The reason for this void may be that the personality of the creating author was too subtle and individual for the imitator to be able to comprehend it and to transfer to his use. The only attribute approaching talent that such an imitative writer can display is the facile ability to paraphrase and reproduce a story or novel of another author just short of actionable plagiarism.

There is no rigid method, by guess or by rule, of evaluating and cataloging a work of fiction regardless of whether it is generally thought of as being authentic art or popular entertainment. Values fluctuate with time and custom. The seesaw of ideals is always in motion. The mere economics of living and the occurrence of social upheavals will divert interests and change concepts overnight. And, perhaps most telling of all, the fresh and vital perspectives of youth are in constant revolt against the precepts of both past and present.

Aside from the usual yearly quota of historical romance and costumed lust, the invasion of another person's privacy provides the essential appeal of contemporary fiction. This is a curiosity to find out what certain persons do, say, think, and otherwise conduct themselves in private and not run the risk of being apprehended and charged with eavesdropping. Every once in a while such novels are written with convincing sincerity, with some basic social substance, with specific implications of good and evil, and narrated in the authentic vernacular of the times.

Unless it is one of those rare and fortunate survivors in the race for literary permanence, the novel that was written in 1900 is likely to have only historical interest for the reader now and beyond. Obviously, after indulging himself in contemporary fiction, the modern reader of a novel written in that past era would consider the style of composition antiquated, the conversations quaint, and the theme and plot unbearably boring and lacking in recognizable romance or reality.

Like fashions in clothing and slang, which change from season to season, the style of the novel has always been in constant revolution. As it has happened in the past, however, it is certain that there will always be readers who will object loudly to any new-placed emphasis or innovation in dialogue and description in a contemporary novel—both now and in the future. Frankness is all right in theory, but there is sure to be somebody to object to it in print.

IV

Learning and training to be a writer has never been easy for anyone, even though there are many inspiring tales in folklore about such-and-such a person having the good fortune to be a natural-born novelist. If any such person ever existed, and actually wrote something, there was one thing he had to acquire by earnest effort and diligent labor before he was able to make use of his talent and get his storytelling into print. It is safe to say, that like anybody else, he had to learn without benefit of natural-born gifts or fortunate genii the ability to put on paper a succession of correctly expressed words and the implications of their meanings.

In order to accomplish such writing, every person has to learn in some way how to tell a story and organize the facts of it in logical sequence; how to dramatize a philosophy of living and convey the implications of conflict; or, for certain other purposes, how to idealize propaganda, to romanticize poverty, or learn how not to offend readers of social items on the society page of the Sunday edition of the newspaper.

Most of the various plans, schemes, systems, and methods of learning to write something for print are seemingly so simple that they could easily be reduced to absurdity. This is because the end result of accomplished writing often appears to be as casual and carefree as child's play.

What the professional writer of fiction or non-fiction knows by experience is that ease of expression and execution of ideas are the result of much more than wishful thinking and the casting of a horoscope.

And yet, no matter how plain and evident the absurdity is there for all to see, hundreds and thousands of persons persist in deluding themselves into believing that authorship is the one profession or craft that requires no training, no study, no aptitude, no skill, no apprenticeship, and no real effort. Of all human aspirations, with the possible exception of the desire for immortality or a reasonable substitute for it, the yearning to attain authorship is the most persistent and time consuming. Nothing else has the constant and compelling lure that writing has as a short-cut to fame and fortune.

Like all attempts to find the reason for such misconceptions, any explanation is bound to be inconclusive. However, it is possible that all such persons with this yearning have seen a certain type of motion picture or television film and were thrilled by the fist fight between the good guy and the bad guy or were titillated by the hair-pulling sequence during which the good girl snatched the bad girl baldheaded. The inference is, of course, that the fiction turned out in great quantity by this enormous portion of the population always seems as if it were written by the same hackneyed hand.

If this is not a satisfactory explanation of the cause of a perennial human hallucination, somebody else will have to think of a better excuse for this type of literary gregariousness. Eventually, of course, psychologists will discover in laboratory experiments with the use of truth serum precisely what ails such people. When the result of these tests is disclosed, it could well be what most of us have suspected from the beginning. But even then it is doubtful if more than a mere handful of these many thousands of fanatical scribblers will take the hint and seek a more humane way of scourging themselves.

Egotistical exhibitionism, physical and literary, has become such a common practice that it is accepted nowadays as a tolerable demonstration of freedom of speech and assembly. Even though not everybody has the physique or personality that warrants exhibition in public, physio-literary exhibitionism has become a flourishing and profitable trade. It should not be surprising then that some young writers, and many who are old enough to know better, have taken to self-flagellation and crying real tears in public, to dredging up their perverted psyche for public display, and to flaunting in print scatological terminology aimed to produce shock waves of notoriety.

Since physio-literary exhibitionism in some form is probably here to stay until times become better, it would be a gracious and much appreciated favor if the practitioner of it would not insist upon reading aloud his poem or essay, his short story or long novel, in the presence of a captive audience. And, if he did go ahead and read it aloud anyway, it would serve him right if he were forced to sit still hour after hour and have to listen to readings of work-in-progress by each and every one of his thirty or forty counterparts in the local physio-literary coterie.

V

There is a brighter side in this summation of authorship. All cannot be dismal and gloomy. There has to be a glimmer of sunlight somewhere.

The dedicated student of writing can see this gleam, because he has confidence in his ability to attain by sincere effort what he sets out to do. He finds encouragement, not in the suspect praise and back-scratching of others, but in his own awareness of his faults and defects as well as accomplishment. This is a personal acknowledgment, and which in itself is the first step toward success, that perfection is elusive and evasive and in constant flight from capture.

To such a perceptive person as this, discouragement never results in prolonged fits of sullen unhappiness and resentment and a bitter surrender to misfortune. Instead, it is put to good use as a goad that drives the ambition to even greater effort. If there is such a thing as inspiration, here is the source of it.

As everybody knows, it is never easy for anyone to be confronted by rejection and failure and to be able to accept it without an ordeal of bitterness and resentment. And yet, when it is recognized that usually the most invaluable lessons are those learned from trials that become errors, each one of them can be converted into profit in the end. The understanding of the causes of errors and failure will be a more valuable and enduring incentive than any accidental or lucky or freakish success in the beginning. There is good reason why there are more one-book authors in the world than any others.

Whether the aim is to make money or to find satisfaction in artistic achievement, or some reasonable combination of both, the long-term capital gain for an industrious author accrues slowly year-by-year throughout a career.

Writing to make money, or, as it is often called in a squeamish rephrasing, writing for profit, is certainly as honorable an occupation as banking, merchandising, manufacturing, or any other legitimate business enterprise. Unfortunately, like any misfit in business, what often happens is that a person will fail to adapt himself and apply his ability to the category of writing for which he is best suited by aptitude and temperament.

One way to determine what to do about all this is for a person to make a realistic test of aptitude and personality. The result of an authentic test has a good possibility of diverting anyone from becoming a poverty-stricken, unsuccessful, embittered, second- or third-rate literary hack. And, as everybody should know, this is already an over-crowded field, even though the common misery of it always makes room for one more.

What this should point to is the fact that writing as an occupation is far from being confined to a select group of persons favored by fate to be the authors of master-pieces of fiction or even passable facsimilies of it.

In other words, the conclusion has to be that any person with the ability to spell reasonably well, with a way of knowing the difference between infinity and infinitive, with a rampant reach for paper and typewriter, with a proclivity for communication, with a surmise of what can be made interesting for information or entertainment, and with all the verve and fervor that a politician can generate —well, a happy combination of these things will give him a fair start.

However, fairness ends abruptly with this beginning. After this it is up to the individual writer to fortify himself against the inevitable, insidious, invidious persecutions of a world full of local book reviewers and professional literary critics. Reviewers and critics have to be tolerated, though; they, too, are writers and as such they are entitled to the privilege of trying to make a living just like anybody else who somehow got into the word business and is trying to make a go of it.

In final summation of the art, craft, and personality of writing, all that remains to be said is that some persons are going to write short stories and novels for other persons to read. Some will be reporting the happenings of life and nature around the corner and around the world. A number of them are going to write the essays of scholarly education and profound learning.

And it would be a dull and humdrum existence for all if somebody did not write the gossip columns, the advice for the lovelorn, the magazine advertisements, the television commercials, the political propaganda, and report the divorce court proceedings for the Sunday newspapers.

THE END